WAUTERS KARIN
Sint. Jorisstraat 3-5
Aalst.

427 CELLEDON
BEAUTIFULL

The Potter's Book of Glaze Recipes

Emmanuel Cooper

B. T. BATSFORD LTD · LONDON

Acknowledgment

The Author would like to thank Gwyneth Newland who worked so hard, conscientiously and so enthusiastically in the preparation of this book — making tests, sorting out recipes, mixing up glazes and firing pots. Without her this book would not have been prepared.

© Emmanuel Cooper 1980
First published 1980
Reprinted 1983

ISBN 0 7134 1996 2

Printed by Butler & Tanner Ltd, Frome and London
for the publishers B T Batsford Limited
4 Fitzhardinge Street, London W1H 0AH

Contents

Introduction

As potters our first experience with glazes comes from either ready prepared glazes sold by commercial firms and mixed by experienced teachers or from glaze recipes culled from potter friends, teachers, books and magazines. From these we work out which glazes we like, what sort of glazes suit our particular requirements or taste, and concentrate on these, using them, experimenting with different glaze thicknesses, adjusting firing temperatures and trying different clays. This book of over 500 glaze recipes and glaze variations is for the potter and student who wants to start with a variety of glazes from which a wide range of effects can be developed. Some are for 'functional' use giving good reliable workable glazes, others offer the potter the opportunity to experiment with a range of glaze effects and decorative surfaces.

Just as the good cook starts with a recipe and then when familiar with it makes it 'individual', so the good potter learns how to handle, control and develop a glaze recipe. Most potters, especially when they are starting out, find the whole process of glazing very difficult. The apparently mysterious ingredients, the intricacies of kiln firing and the sheer spectacle of the dull dry powdery mixtures being transformed by terrific heat into attractive, or sometimes unattractive, glazes seem overwhelming. Some teachers and potters also have a puritan attitude which insists that potters should develop their own glazes; such an argument ignores the fact that potters have been developing glazes for centuries and from them we learn a great deal and build upon their knowledge. What better starting point than a book of glaze recipes?

From recipes we can learn how materials behave, what effect the ingredients have on each other and on the various colouring oxides. By simple adjustments with the ingredients the glaze can be made either more shiny, more matt, more opaque: maturing temperatures can be lowered or made higher.

In this book the glazes are divided into 5 sections according to the firing temperature required. Within each section the glazes are further divided into various groups according to how they appear when fired — that is in transparent, matt, opaque, coloured and other glaze groups, so that the potter can refer easily to the section required. Some glazes require such materials as wood ash and natural local clays, and where these are unobtainable similar substitutes must be made: the recipes here act as useful starting points, for potters must first test out their own materials and results will inevitably vary. However, such glazes often have rich decorative surfaces unobtainable by any other means. As such the recipes give the potter a well tried basic recipe with which to work.

There is also a large group of glazes which gives good results over a wide temperature range. With the increased awareness about dwindling fossil fuels and the increased cost of obtaining them, potters, along with other members of society, are very conscious of the need for energy conservation. Most potters prefer to fire to stoneware temperature when the body becomes vitrified and stronger and the glaze effects more varied, but they also want to achieve these effects at as low a temperature as possible. For this reason, this wide firing range of glazes is of particular interest. At 1200°C (2192°F) most bodies are almost vitrified and all these glazes give good workable results. At higher temperatures the glaze changes, but sometimes not drastically so, and these glazes extend the glazer's range in many ways.

All potters' materials vary slightly from batch to batch, and from source to source. The suppliers take great care to provide materials with as consistent an analysis as possible, but even they cannot eliminate all the slight 'impurities' nature has introduced. For this reason it is sensible to test all recipes with your materials before large batches of glaze are made: if inconsistencies occur then a slight adjustment may be necessary. In the chapter on glaze preparation and adjustment, guidance is provided on how this can be done successfully.

All the recipes given in this book include descriptions of the glazes. Some are full and detailed, others are much shorter where no further explanation is necessary. But they are my own descriptions and may not match up to the glaze as it comes out in other firings. The earthenware glazes have been fired on a red earthenware body, the medium stoneware glazes on a red earthenware body, a medium stoneware body and on porcelain. All the stoneware glazes have been fired on a medium coloured stoneware body and on porcelain. Descriptions relate to these fired results. On lighter or darker coloured bodies colours and surface qualities vary. However precise the recipe and however careful the description and preparation, it is always necessary for each potter to test the glaze using his own glaze materials, clays and kilns before mixing up big batches.

The Glaze Materials

Almost all the materials used in this book have been obtained from pottery suppliers and are generally reliably obtainable though materials do vary from supplier to supplier and from batch to batch. Few potters are able or find it necessary to collect their own materials, though there are locally available materials (such as wood ash) which the potter does like to use. Glazes are made up of three different sorts of materials — fluxes which make the glaze melt, the amphoteric or stabilizing materials which give the glaze 'flesh', and acidic oxides which are the glass forming part or 'bone' of the glaze. With only a few exceptions, most glaze materials are mixtures and combinations of materials from each of these groups, and a check through the recipes will show that most glazes include them. From the point of view of economy, the range of materials has been kept to a minimum, but many minerals do offer their own qualities, though substitutes can often be made.

All the glaze materials supplied by the pottery manufacturers are washed and finely ground. Some come as a fine powder (most have been passed through a 300 mesh sieve), some as lumps, but all are ready for use. Other materials like wood ash, granite or local clay need special preparation, and this is explained below, but other materials can be used as supplied. They should be stored in containers, clearly labelled with the name of the material as well as the date on which it was bought, and the name of the supplier.

Materials which come about naturally and can be collected and prepared by the potter have a fascination both for their cheapness and their unique qualities, yet, it is these qualities which make them unreliable to quote in glaze recipes. For this reason tests are always essential. It is not possible here to describe all the variations and the different effects that can be obtained, but there are a few useful points about their preparation.

Wood Ash
Wood ash is perhaps the most variable — and most useful. The sort of tree, shrub or plant, the soil in which it was grown, and even the time of year at which the plant was cut down are all factors which will affect the content of the ash. Ideally ash should be well burnt — either in a

hearth or bonfire, and all the fine particles collected and carefully stored in a lidded container.

The ash can be used as an ordinary glaze ingredient in this unwashed state with the bits of carbon and unburnt wood still present. Most of these will be removed when the glaze is sieved, and this ash will make a much more speckled glaze. Alternatively the ash can be carefully prepared by washing and sieving beforehand by putting it carefully into a large bucket of water and stirring well. The unburnt wood and carbon will float to the top and the fine ash will slowly settle. After a few hours the water will dissolve the soluble salts of potassium and sodium and become a pale yellow colour; the water should be poured or syphoned off.

This procedure needs to be repeated three times if the ash is to be washed properly. This mixture, using plenty of water, should be passed through an 80 mesh sieve and allowed to settle. As much of the water should be removed as possible, and the ash sludge should be allowed to dry out; a good method is to place it inside a biscuit-fired bowl. The dry ash should be stored inside a labelled lidded container. Mixed ash from bonfires or hearths is most common (and this is what has been used in these recipes), but occasionally it is possible to obtain 'single' ashes like oak, apple or privet, all of which give distinct qualities in the glaze.

Local Clays

Local clays are prepared in much the same way. They should be dried out completely, broken up into small lumps and these dropped into plenty of hot water. When they have slaked down, the clay slip should be thoroughly mixed up and the mixture put through an 80 mesh sieve. When this has settled, which will be a slow process (about 2–3 days) depending on the fineness of the particles, the water should be removed and the slip put to dry.

Most local clays, particularly those rich in iron (average 8%) make excellent glaze materials — Albany slip clay, found near Albany, New York, is a famous example. A good clay slip will melt on its own at around 1250°C (2282°F) to form a dark coloured (usually brown or black) shiny glaze and can be used in glaze recipes to excellent effect. Unfortunately few local clays have the necessary small particle size to melt so well. This can be remedied by grinding the dry clay in a pestle and mortar — a slow process. A better method, if the equipment is available, is to mill the clay in a ball mill from three to four hours, which makes the clay much more fusable. The Fremington clay used in these recipes was ball milled for four hours.

Rocks

Rocks, particularly granites or slates, are another cheap and often fascinating source. These are best collected from granite quarries where fine dust often lies around sawing machines. When collected this is often sufficiently fine to use as it is. Otherwise it requires grinding or ball milling. Different outcrops will of course vary in composition and each batch must be tested.

Glaze Temperature and Classification

There are many different ways of classifying glazes — according to the ingredients, the colour, the opacity of the glaze or even the use to which the glaze will be put. The most common method and perhaps the clearest and most easily understood is to divide the glazes up according to temperature at which they mature, which is the method I have used here. Glazes fall into three main groups — low temperature $1000°C$–$1150°C$ ($1832°F$–$2102°F$) for earthenware pots, medium temperature $1200°C$–$1220°C$ ($2192°F$–$2228°F$) for stoneware, and high temperature $1250°C$–$1280°C$ ($2282°F$–$2336°F$) for stoneware and porcelain. A fourth group includes those glazes which have a wide firing range $1200°C$–$1260°C$ ($2192°F$–$2300°F$). Most glazes can successfully be coloured or stained by additions of metal colouring oxides: where this has resulted in attractive effects this will also be mentioned and many of the possibilities listed, but not all the recipes have been tested with every variation of colouring oxide, and potters could experiment with prepared glazes for other effects.

Within each group, glazes are divided under sub-headings starting with transparent and semi-transparent, opaque and matt, coloured, and iron glazes. Glazes which are not easily classified have been added at the end of each section as 'special effects'.

Colouring Glazes

Many potters when they have discovered a range of good workable glazes often prefer to experiment with them rather than keep trying out different glazes. For instance, a reliable shiny clear glaze can be easily opacified by the addition of tin oxide or zirconium silicate. Such a glaze can also be coloured by adding metal oxides, underglaze colour or glaze stain. This section describes how various effects and colours can be obtained. It is necessary to point out, however, that glaze colours are affected very much by different conditions and factors. In the first instance the colour depends on the body of the pot, and how much iron it contains. Accordingly this will either darken or brighten the glaze. On white firing and porcelain bodies, colours will generally be brighter. Some bodies 'suck in' the colour and glaze to leave a roughish surface, while others, particularly the highly vitrified bodies, will render these glazes smooth and even.

The glaze colour and quality are also affected by the firing atmosphere of the kiln, whether it is oxidized or reduced. These differences in effect are described in the recipe notes.

The temperature reached, the length of firing and the thickness of the glaze application are also important considerations which affect the final appearance of the glaze. It is, therefore, essential to test the glaze with your own materials, on your own clay, and in your own kiln, to find out exactly how it will respond to individual conditions.

White Glazes

Tin oxide (SnO_2) will make most shiny glazes opaque, and an addition of 8%–12% will give a clear, cool blue-white.

Zirconium silicate ($ZrSio_4$) ('Zircon'), which is a less refined form of zirconium oxide, is used as an opacifier; 6%–15% is required to give a neutral or cream white.

Coloured Glazes

Chromium oxide (Cr_2O_3) in most glazes gives an opaque green glaze with additions of 0.5%–2%. In some glazes crimson red is obtained with the chrome-tin-pink combination.

Cobalt carbonate ($CoCO_3$) produces a smooth blue glaze varying from pink mauve (in a dolomite glaze), and vivid blue in an alkaline glaze to midnight blue in a feldspathic glaze; additions range from 0.5%–3%, and results are not affected strongly by reduction or oxidation atmospheres.

Cobalt oxide (CoO) gives colour similar to cobalt carbonate but is, weight for weight, more powerful. The oxide tends to be less evenly distributed in the glaze and can cause blue specks.

Copper carbonate (CuCO₃) produces colours which range from pink (in dolomite glazes) and red (in reduction atmospheres) to green (in lead glazes) or brilliant turquoise (in alkaline glazes). Amounts required in the glaze range from 0.5% (for copper reds in reduction) to 2% (for alkaline turquoise in oxidation) to 4% for strong greens (in lead glazes).

Copper oxide (CuO) is almost exactly the same as the carbonate but is weight for weight much more powerful. Note that both copper carbonate and copper oxide tend to encourage the release of lead in lead glazes during the glaze firing making the lead soluble in acid solutions. For this reason lead glazes, particularly those with copper addition, should not be used on the inside of vessels used for holding food and drink of any kind.

Iron oxide, Black (FeO) and Red (Fe₂O₃) The black iron oxide is, weight for weight, more powerful than the red, but in most glazes better results are achieved with the synthetic red iron oxide. Depending on the amount of oxide added to the glaze (1%–15%) and the firing atmosphere, the colour may range from pale blue green to brown black red in reduction, and range from pale honey to olive brown or black red in oxidation, in feldspathic glazes. In the dolomite glazes colour tends to be more muddy and muted. Iron oxide can act as flux, particularly at the higher temperatures, and may cause glazes to run. A substitution of weight for weight iron oxide and a flux will combat this, but often the quality of a black brown tenmoku glaze depends on it 'running' on the pot.

Manganese carbonate (MnCO₃) gives pink mauve colours in alkaline and dolomite glazes and browns in feldspathic glazes, using 1%–8%.

Manganese dioxide (MnO₂) gives results similar to the carbonate but is, weight for weight, more powerful.

Nickel oxide (NiO) gives colours ranging from ice blue (with zinc oxide glazes), yellow (with zinc oxide and titanium dioxide), pink and mauve (with barium carbonate and zinc oxide) to muted greens and greys in most ordinary glazes. Amounts added range from 1%–3%.

Rutile (FeTiO₃) (Light, medium and dark), sometimes called rutile sand, is an ore containing titanium with iron oxide. It gives buff or brown colours in oxidation in glazes which can be mottled or crystalline, and it opacifies the glaze. In reduction rich blue grey colours can be achieved. Amounts added may be 2%–15%.

Titanium dioxide (TiO_2) gives glazes a matt creamy white colour in oxidation, and is often used in crystalline glazes. In reduction it gives a rich blue grey mottled effect; 2%–10% can be added.

Uranium oxide (U_3O_8) gives yellows and reds in amounts of 2%–5%. Being slightly radio-active, it needs storing in a metal container.

Vanadium pentoxide (V_2O_5) gives colours ranging from yellow to brown and tends to break up the glaze, added in amounts of 3%–8%.

Yellow ochre (Fe_2O_3) is a natural form of 'iron' oxide containing clay, and gives similar effects in the glaze.

Mixing the Glaze

For the sake of safety it is best if all ingredients are stored in clearly labelled bins, buckets or jars with lids. This means that dust is controlled and half-empty packets or sacks of material do not issue clouds of their powdery contents when disturbed. Potters need always to bear in mind the toxicity of the glaze materials they use. Most are perfectly safe but some are poisonous if eaten or inhaled even in small quantities. For instance any form of lead, most metal oxides and barium carbonate should all be labelled 'poisonous'. Good housekeeping — wet washing of surfaces and tools, regular vacuum cleaning, smooth surfaces and so on will also reduce or eliminate any possible hazard. Common sense, care and control in the handling and use of glaze materials as well as with other materials cannot be emphasized too strongly.

Glazes are made up by carefully mixing weighed ingredients into water, then passing the mixture through a fine sieve to break up the lumps and provide a thorough homogeneous mixture. For ease of mixing and comparing ingredients all the recipes total 100 parts: oxide additions are listed as percentage additions to the total. Depending on the amount of glaze that is required, the quantities can be interpreted as grams or ounces; 100 grams will produce enough glaze to fill a small glass jar or yoghurt pot, 1000 grams will be enough for a large bucket.

Scales need to be sufficiently large to hold good sized amounts of materials. Balance kitchen scales are more accurate than spring scales, especially for measuring small amounts. For weighing out quantities for test glazes a small accurate balance is required — chemical or photographic balances are ideal, though special balances, usually quite expensive in price, are marketed by the pottery manufacturers. But any accurate set of scales will suffice. Occasionally old fashioned confectionery scales can be purchased cheaply in second-hand or junk shops.

Plastic buckets or bowls are ideal for mixing and containing the glaze — they are light in weight, quiet in use and easy to clean. Sizes vary from small 'honey tubs' (often cheaply obtainable from confectioners) to a standard household bucket. For glazes required in large quantities small waste bins or plastic dustbins can be purchased from hardware stores. Quantities of glaze are important for they determine the way pots are to be glazed. For instance the workshop potter will probably prefer to dip the pots in glaze, so a good sized barrel with plenty of glaze is required. For the potter working on a small scale smaller amounts of glaze may seem more desirable, but this does limit the method of glaze application which can only be applied either by pouring the glaze or painting it on the pot. Glaze can also be sprayed but this does need specialist and expensive equipment. All these methods are discussed in the section on glaze application.

To mix the glaze weigh out the dry ingredients and gently add these to water. Tick off the amounts on the recipe when they are added to the water; this helps to eliminate mistakes while mixing. The water helps to break up the ingredients, which should be left in the water to 'slake' down. Lumps will break down and within a few hours a thick uneven sludge will form in the bottom of the barrel. Mix this up with the liquid so that a thinnish watery mixture is formed. This mixture should now be put twice through an 80 mesh sieve using a glaze brush or a domestic washing-up brush. This process will break up any tiny lumps and form a homogeneous, evenly mixed glaze. Ensure that as much glaze material passes through the sieve as possible.

At this stage the glaze, too thin to use on pots, should be allowed to settle. To test this for glaze thickness, dip a finger or a piece of bis-cuited pot into the well stirred mixture. If the glaze runs off it is too thin. Allow the glaze to settle so that the ingredients sink to the bottom. Depending on the ingredients of the glaze this will take from one to twenty four hours. High clay glazes for instance are slower to settle, while materials high in non-plastic ingredients like frits will settle quickly.

Remove plenty of clear water from the top, either by carefully ladling it out or by syphoning it off with a rubber tube. Thoroughly mix up the glaze using either your hand or a large kitchen swish. Again test for thickness. For pouring or dipping the pot, the glaze should have the thickness of single cream. It should give the hand a good coating and as a general guide it should form a thickness of glaze on the pot which, when dry, can be scratched to leave a clean and identifiable mark.

Different glazes require different thicknesses; choice will depend on personal preference. Some glazes change in colour and texture when they are thicker and it is always worthwhile checking this with a single and a double thickness. Potters who want a more scientific test of glaze thickness can use a hydrometer which measures the density (known as the specific gravity, SG) of the mixture. A simple instrument can be made by weighing a length of wood about 30 cm (12 in) long at one end. Drop this into the mixed glaze when it is at the consistency required and mark on the stick with waterproof paint the point where it goes into the glaze. On subsequent occasions if the glaze is too thin the mark will disappear below the surface; if it is too thick the mark will be above the surface.

An alternative method is to check the weight of the glaze. An empty glass jar with a volume of 1 kg or 1 lb is first weighed and then filled with glaze of the correct consistency and weighed again, then the original weight of the empty jar is subtracted. For an average glaze, for use on porous biscuit, 1500 grams to a litre (31½ ounces to a pint) is approximately correct. For glaze which is to be applied to a more vitrified body a higher density, about 1600 grams to a litre (34 ounces to a pint) is necessary. These weights are only approximate guides, for it is the prepared thickness which is important. Equally a glaze which is to be applied raw to unfired pots may have to be even thicker.

All glazes listed in this book have a quantity of a plastic material such as ball clay or bentonite in the recipe to help glaze suspension and to help bind the glaze when it is dry but not yet fired. This makes the glaze easier to handle as it is less likely to chip or dust off the surface. Some glazes, particularly those with large amounts of non-plastic materials like nepheline syenite or Cornish stone, settle in the glaze barrel very quickly and may form a hard layer which is difficult to break up. Such glazes will often be made easier to handle by the addition of a few drops of water in which either calcium chloride or sodium chloride have been mixed. Only small quantities are required. This mixture has the effect of 'thickening' the glaze, but add this very carefully as too much will turn the glaze into an unusable jelly-like consistency.

Glazes should be stored in lidded containers and of course should be clearly and properly labelled. Some potters make little 'button' glaze tests on round clay discs and tie these onto the bucket as a visual reminder of the glaze qualities. This is particularly useful for the experimental potter who is constantly involved in glaze tests.

Applying the Glaze

All the glazes listed in this book have been used on porous biscuit fired clay first fired to low biscuit temperature 980°C (1796°F). Many glazes, particularly those with a high clay content, can be used on raw unfired clay. These glazes will be indicated as such. All the comments refer to glaze applied in normal thickness unless marked otherwise.

The majority of studio potters apply their glaze by dipping the pot into it. This is quick, efficient and, provided there is sufficient glaze and the pot is handled well, gives an even covering of glaze. Areas which are required to be glaze free, like flanges and galleries, lids, or foot rings, can be painted either with hot wax or a water-based wax emulsion which will resist the glaze. When the glaze slop is well stirred, which with highly plastic ingredients can be a relatively slow process, the mixture should be checked for thickness and adjusted accordingly.

To dip, the pot should be held firmly, either on the foot ring or on the rim and foot ring, depending on the size of the pot, and dipped into the glaze. Depending on the thickness of the walls (thin walled pots need to be dipped more quickly) the pot should be left in the glaze for about three seconds, and should be gently moved around while it is in the glaze. Lift it out holding it upside down to drain thoroughly. Make sure no trapped air pockets have caused 'blind' spots of glaze inside the pot; when the surface has lost its shine it can be gently handled and the pot put aside to dry. Dab on glaze where the fingers have left scar marks or tiny bald patches on the rim or any other place. Avoid touching the pot any more than is necessary until it is quite dry.

Thin walled pots or pots which are to be glazed inside and outside with different glazes should have glaze poured first on the inside. Leave this to dry for several hours so if the walls have become completely saturated they can dry out. Any runs or dribbles of glaze on the outside should be sponged, scratched or rubbed off. The outside can now be glazed either by dipping the inverted pot, kept horizontal, into the glaze, or the outside can be glazed by pouring. For large pots or when only a small amount of glaze is available, pouring is a useful method. Insides of containers can be swilled out rapidly with glaze and the excess poured out. Speed is important if an even layer is to be obtained.

Pouring glaze on the outside also has to be done fairly quickly. On small pots this is no problem; the pot should be held over a bowl and glaze poured liberally from a jug down the sides. Large pots need to be stood on glaze sticks over a bowl, and the glaze poured evenly round the pot. Aim for full flow effects to ensure the covering is regular.

After being glazed the pots must be prepared for the kiln and this varies according to the pot and temperature. Earthenware pots are often glazed all over, inside, outside and underneath and stood on stilts, 'spurs' or triangular points in the kiln. These are removed with a swift tap after the firing, and the tiny glaze scars smoothed over with a carborundum stone. Because of the sharp and dangerous edges round the glaze scar it is essential that this is done.

Pots taken to a higher temperature, when the body becomes non-porous, are best fired by being stood directly on the kiln shelf. The shelf should first be dusted lightly with alumina hydrate to prevent the pot sticking to it and to enable the pot to move across the shelf as it contracts. At stoneware temperature most clay bodies soften slightly (and become pyroplastic) and if stood on stilts would distort. Furthermore most bodies become non-porous around 1200°C (2192°F) and so do not absorb water on non-glazed areas. Foot rings and the base of the pots need to be cleaned of glaze either by scratching off the glaze or sponging it off with water.

Glaze also needs to be removed from the bottom of the wall, though the amount to wipe off depends on the viscosity of the glaze. A stiff glaze needs to be cleaned off by about 3 mm ($\frac{1}{8}$ in) while a runny glaze needs a much greater distance. This is particularly necessary for shiny crystalline glazes which depend for their success on the glaze moving over the surface of the pot. Such glazes need special attention both in their application (correct thickness is vital) and in their placing in the kiln; in too hot a spot the glaze will run too much, too cool and no crystals will form. It is also a wise precaution to place pots with these sorts of glazes on a pad of clay or on a layer of alumina sand to catch any glaze runs.

Besides dipping and pouring, glaze can be applied by painting or spraying. Both methods have their advantages. Painted glaze, unless it is in very small areas, needs to be applied in several coats with a broad brush, each layer being allowed to dry before the next is applied. Gum arabic added to the glaze mixture will bind the layer onto the pot and enable this to be done. One of the main advantages of paint application is the small quantity of glaze required; the mixture can be applied to either biscuit fired, non-fired or even vitrified pots; a further advantage is that the layers can be built up so that if desired a thicker layer than usual can be applied than by pouring or dipping.

Spraying glaze, a method common in industry, also has special advantages. For instance, glaze can be applied to a vitrified surface and can be used to cover large areas quickly; the spray can also be used for graduations of colour. Also, only small amounts of glaze are necessary. Suitable equipment is essential: a spray gun and compressor, and a spray booth with an extractor fan with an outside exhaust. The fine airborne glaze spray should not be breathed in, nor should the glaze be allowed to settle on working surfaces; ideally a water curtain should trap any glaze and the spray booth outlet should be well away from the workshop. Glaze to be sprayed needs to be sieved through a 120 mesh sieve so that the spray nozzle does not become blocked. Some glazes, particularly if they have colouring oxides in them, benefit from being ground in a pestle and mortar or, better still, milled for a couple of hours to ensure even distribution of colour and avoid 'specking'.

Pots which are vitrified should be heated first to enable the sprayed glaze to dry more quickly from the surface. To use the spray, place the pot in the spray booth on a banding wheel and with the gun held 30–45 cm (12–18 in) away, glaze the pot with short bursts directed evenly round the pot as the wheel is slowly rotated. Do not direct the spray in one spot or the glaze will run. Build up a normal thickness of glaze ensuring that all the surfaces underneath handles, inside ridges and so on are properly coated. Estimating the surface thickness is more difficult with sprayed glazes but it can be tested by scratching it with a pin.

Any thin or bald patches must be touched up with glaze; a large, floppy, soft-bristled glaze mop will blob on the correct amount. It is necessary to put more on than first seems necessary as when it dries it halves in thickness and any surplus can be gently rubbed down with the finger. Any runs or dribbles on the glaze surface can be gently rubbed down to make an even coat. Where lids are fired in place on the pot check that touching surfaces are clean and free from glaze and that glaze has been cleaned back from the edge so that the problem of 'sticking-in', caused by the glaze running into the seating, will be avoided. A thin wash of alumina sand and china clay painted in the galley will prevent the surfaces sticking together, and can be rubbed off with a carborundum stone after firing.

Adjusting the Glaze

No recipe is infallible. Materials, bodies, firing conditions and so on vary and give slightly different results. It is necessary to have as much information about a glaze recipe as possible so that, if necessary, adjustments can be made. All the glaze recipes in this book have been used as described and the results obtained are detailed. Listed here are many practical, reliable recipes which give quieter, stable glazes; there are also recipes which are more spectacular in effect. These latter glazes depend for their success on more precise firing conditions, and simple adjustments to the glaze recipe can be made which will help to make them work for slightly different conditions. All the glazes can be modified, and general notes and suggestions for this are listed below.

Runny glaze

A glaze which runs freely and causes the pot to adhere to the kiln shelf has either been applied too thickly or fired too high or soaked too long at top temperature. The remedy is the opposite of all these causes. Alternatively the glaze must be 'stiffened', or made less viscous by the addition of equal parts of china clay and flint to the glaze recipe; a starting point would be 3–5% by weight of each material. This may of course affect the appearance of the glaze, and is a factor which must be borne in mind especially for crystalline or special effect glazes, when a low alumina content is essential. In this case it may be more useful to reduce the thickness of the glaze and slightly lower the firing temperature. Pots with glazes which have run freely can be ground off at the bottom, then reglazed and refired to a lower temperature.

Dry pinholed glaze surface

When a glaze melts it goes through many changes depending on the type and the content of the glaze. Shiny glazes, high in fluxes, melt dramatically, and bubble before evening out to form a clear glass. In contrast glazes which are more matt and opaque are often high in china clay and flint, both of which stabilize the glaze. In these glazes the melting and maturing process takes place over a longer period and over a wider temperature range. Bubbles and so on are slower to clear. If temperature has been too low or too rapidly reached such glazes may be dry with pinholes; here the remedy is simply a slightly higher temperature or a longer soak at top temperature. Some glazes, particularly those which respond to reducing conditions, develop rich surfaces only when fully reduced. An under-reducing firing leaves them fluxed but dull in colour and quality.

If the temperature cannot be raised, then the glaze may benefit from a slightly increased amount of flux (the material that makes the glaze melt). This may be done either by reducing slightly the amounts of china clay and flint or increasing the fluxes in the recipe, such as whiting or dolomite. Alternatively small amounts (3-4%) of a secondary flux may be introduced, such as alkaline frit or calcium borate frit. Gerstley borate or colemanite may be substituted for the frit. In these quantities the glaze temperature is effectively lowered without the quality of the glaze being drastically affected. Glazes on pots which have not reached temperature can be fired again.

Bubbled and cratered glaze

As described earlier, glazes go through a complex series of changes and reactions which are not necessarily stopped when the temperature is reached, when the glaze is said to be matured: the surface may continue to even out and smooth over and, depending on the rate of cooling, crystals may form. However, if the temperature goes on rising then the ingredients continue to react much more violently and, just as for example when a sugar solution is overheated it boils and burns, so a glaze can boil and bubble. So violent is this process that part of the glaze is given off as vapour and the glaze will not settle down; the result is a rough glaze surface often displaying craters with jagged edges. Incidentally this sort of glaze surface must not be confused with crater glazes which are deliberately sought effects which have cratered surface but are smooth with no jagged edges.

Bubbled and cratered glaze surfaces can be avoided by firing to a lower temperature or have a shorter soak period. Alternatively additions of china clay and flint to the glaze will rise the maturing temperature. On pots where overfiring has occurred the surface can be rubbed over with a carborundum stone and a further layer of glaze can be applied by gently heating the pot first, and refiring.

Crazing

The balance of the glaze between the glaze layer and the body of the pot is crucial to a well fitting and strong glaze. During the firing the glaze slowly melts and 'bites' into the surface of the pot to form a 'layer of interaction' between the glaze and the clay. Depending on the glaze ingredients this layer is either indistinct (as for example in an ash glaze) or, in glassy glazes, the glaze and body are two fairly distinct layers. In this sort of glaze the expansion of the glaze and the body should be more or less equal if a well fitting glaze is to be achieved. If the glaze has a large proportion of high expansion fluxes, such as sodium and potassium, they cause the glaze to expand greatly while it is melted: as the glaze cools these fluxes cause it to contract, often more than the body of the pot. When this happens the glaze develops fine hair-like cracks over its surface which effectively spreads and stretches it over the pot. This is a particularly bad fault on earthenware pots which are not vitrified as the craze lines allow moisture to be absorbed through the surface, into the pot. On domestic pots it may also be unhygienic. The remedy here is to biscuit fire the pot to a higher temperature to make the pot less porous.

On stoneware pots crazing is not so important from the hygienic point of view, but it does make the pot physically less strong. The comparison here is with plywood, where two layers give strength to the other. If one layer cracks and breaks up the other layer is drastically weakened. On functional pots which are handled frequently, crazing is a weakness.

On pots which are more decorative, such an effect can be very attractive and is known as crackle. The Chinese potters were masters of this technique. Depending on the glaze and position in the kiln, various crackle effects could be achieved, from long slender lined crackles to tiny angular islands. Often finely ground colouring oxides or inks were rubbed into the surface to heighten the crackle effect. To connoisseurs the crackle was an important aspect of the pot.

When crazing is a problem, the glaze has to be 'stiffened' to stop it melting so freely. Either the high expansion alkaline fluxes have to be replaced by those of lower expansion such as magnesia or lithium or the amount of flint has to be increased. A practical suggestion is to add small amounts of talc (a mineral consisting of magnesium and flint) to the glaze.

Other remedies are to fire the glaze to a different temperature, either slightly lower or higher. Amounts of boron added to the glaze in the form of calcium borate or gerstley borate will also help to correct this.

Shivering, shelling or peeling

Glaze which flakes off the pot at the rims, on the edge of handles, or on raised decoration, is the opposite problem to crazing and is known as shivering, shelling or peeling. It occurs during the cooling period when the body contracts more than the glaze putting it under slight compression which gives the pot great strength. For all practical purposes this is the 'ideal' situation. However, when this compression is too great the glaze is literally forced off the rims of the pot or edges of the handles as flakes or slivers of glaze. This may happen as the pot cools, as it is taken from the kiln or after a period of days or weeks. It is dangerous, for the glaze slivers may fall into food, and it is unsightly. In severe cases the compression may literally cause the pot to split into several pieces.

The cure is basically the opposite of that suggested for crazing and is aimed at making the glaze contract more on cooling. This is achieved by substituting high expansion fluxes for those with lower expansion and reducing the amount of flint. In practice, the flint can be replaced by feldspar or by alkaline fluxes. I have found that lowering the firing temperature also helps to correct this maddening fault; particularly irritating in this respect are some glazes high in iron oxide.

Dunting, cracking or spiral cracking

Pots can crack in the glaze firing for two main reasons. The first reason, shivering, has already been dealt with. The second, commonly called dunting, occurs when a pot is cooled too quickly either by a cool draught of air or because the door of the kiln is opened too soon. It is rare in electric kilns and more common in flame burning kilns. The crack often takes the form of a spiral round the pot, usually picking out the weakest point such as where the wall is slightly thinner or where the base and sides join. Too great a compression of the glaze will also encourage this to happen.

Dunting as opposed to other forms of cracking can be recognized by the characteristic of the crack: if it is a clean split showing clear distinctions between body and glaze layer the crack has occurred after the glaze has matured. Cracks which were present before glazing and firing will show smoother edges where the matured glaze has healed over the edges.

Draughts of any sort must be avoided. Kilns should not be 'cracked' or opened until 200°C (392°F), and kiln doors not disturbed until 100°C (212°F). The top damper can safely be opened at 400°C (752°F), never earlier. Spy holes should remain firmly clammed up so no through draughts are created. A further precaution is to ensure that the pot is glazed on both the inside and the outside so compression on both sides of the wall is equal.

Crawling

Glaze which forms into rolls and lumps, leaving bare patches on the surface of the clay, known as crawling, has two basic causes — dust or shrinkage of the glaze. Some glazes, particularly those containing tin oxide, if applied too thickly or over a dusty surface will crawl up into large fat lumps. The remedy here is to ensure that the pots are dust free by wet sponging the surface. Avoid blowing off the dust, unless in a dust extraction booth, as this should not be inhaled. If the glaze needs a thick application a small percentage (3%) of bentonite can be added to the glaze mixture. This sort of crawling can also happen over painted or sprayed underglaze decoration which acts like dust under the glaze. In this case a small amount of glaze or gum arabic needs to be mixed into the underglaze powder to bind it onto the pot.

The second major cause is a glaze which is too high in plastic ingredients: during drying the glaze contracts and forms small craze lines which break up the surface. During the firing these glaze 'islands' do not melt to form an allover covering but go into lumps: this usually happens on biscuit fired pots. Such glazes can usually be successfully applied raw, that is directly onto unfired or green ware; they can be adapted for use on biscuit fired work by substituting non-plastic clay such as calcined clay, either molochite (china clay) or calcite (ball clay), weight for weight for plastic clay. Gently rubbing the dry surface of the glaze with the finger to smooth over and fill-in any cracks can also help. Rapidly heating the glaze before it has dried out slowly will also cause 'islands' to form.

Bloating

Bubbles or lumps which occur in the body of the fired body of the pot, which when broken, show no evidence of foreign matter, are known as bloats. They usually only occur at high temperature, either because the body is overfired (in which case there are many smaller lumps) or when carbon is trapped in the body. Carbon from the remains of plants and rotting vegetation are present in all clay bodies, to a greater or lesser extent. During the biscuit or first firing, the carbon burns away as carbon dioxide or carbon monoxide from 500°C (932°F) to 900°C (1652°F). During this period the firing must be sufficiently slow and with enough oxygen present to allow complete combustion of the carbon to take place; this is a slower process on pots with thicker walls. If the firing is too rapid, the walls of the pot begin to vitrify and prevent the carbon gases from escaping or the heat does not soak through sufficiently; during the later glaze firing the trapped carbon turns into gas and expands and as the body softens causes a bloat or bubble to form; sometimes the surface is split.

The remedy here is to fire the body to a lower temperature or, more practically, slow down the speed of the biscuit firing. Many potters 'soak' their kiln at 900°C (1652°F) for one to two hours to enable all carbon to be burnt off. Some clays have a higher carbon content than others, and kilns can emit quite thick clouds of slightly blue and acrid tasting smoke. Ventilation to remove these gases is essential, as in too large quantities they are quite dangerous and a build up of the gas can occur slowly if sufficient precautions are not taken.

Health and Safety

All materials used by the potter should never be inhaled or ingested, for all are to some extent harmful. The actual degree of toxicity depends on the particular material, how finely it has been ground and the amount taken into the body. Some are more poisonous than others; for example, nickel oxide, zinc oxide, copper oxide, copper carbonate, chromium oxide, barium carbonate, flint and lead bisilicate all require special care in handing, but with a commonsense approach danger can be avoided. Good housekeeping will deal with the problems:

(1) Keep all materials in properly labelled bins, jars or holders with well-fitting lids.
(2) When mixing glazes always add glaze materials to water, gently letting them slide into the water; avoid dropping them and so creating dust.
(3) Work in a well ventilated room.
(4) Wipe up any spilled glaze material or splashed glaze with a damp cloth. Wash off all utensils before they dry out to avoid dust contamination.
(5) Scrub hands, particularly nails, after mixing and handling glaze.
(6) Do not eat or drink while mixing glazes.

Lead

The superiority of lead glazes for the earthenware potter lies in their brilliance, lustre and smoothness; unfortunately lead is a poisonous material and most countries have special regulations governing its use. Most potters are now aware of the dangers in the use of lead. As a raw material it is a poison which, if taken into the body through the mouth, the lungs, or absorbed through cuts or scratches, builds up in the body and is difficult to break down and release. For this reason the raw forms of lead are avoided in the workshop and lead frits are used instead. Lead bisilicate is the safest form.

In a fired glaze lead can also be soluble in weak acid solutions where there is an imbalance in the construction of the glaze. For this reason it is best to avoid lead glazes on vessels intended to store or serve food or drink, unless they have first been tested for lead solubility at an established and reputable laboratory.

The Glaze Recipes

All the recipes are listed as parts by weight, and amounts are expressed as percentages. All the glaze ingredients are listed with the fluxes first then the clays and finally the flint. Additions to the basic glaze recipes are expressed as percentage parts by weight over and above the basic glaze; such materials are listed at the bottom of the recipe.

All of the materials are easily obtained from pottery suppliers (except for local materials) but variations do occur and batches should be tested first. Where feldspar is included in the recipe, this refers to potash feldspar. Where soda feldspar is required this is specifically mentioned. Feldspars in the United States often have names or numbers, and direct substitutions can be made according to type. The list of materials at the end of the book gives the full range of equivalents available in the USA. Where materials are included in brackets in the recipes, this is to indicate close American equivalents.

Earthenware Glazes 1050 °C - 1100 °C (1922 °F - 2012 °F) Orton cones 04 or 03

Transparent glazes

---

1 **Clear glaze**

Calcium borate frit (Colemanite)	65
Red clay	35

A clear, well fitting glaze.

---

2 **Standard clear glaze**

Lead bisilicate (Ferro 3498)	85
Cornish stone	15

A good, clear, rich glaze.

Variation
With an addition of 2% red iron oxide a pale honey coloured transparent glaze results.

---

3 **Clear glaze**

Lead bisilicate (Ferro 3498)	60

Feldspar (soda)	15
Cornish stone	15
Whiting	5
Zinc oxide	5

A reliable, clear glaze.

---

4   Clear glaze

| Lead bisilicate (Ferro 3498) | 80 |
| Ball clay | 20 |

A simple, clear glaze.

---

5   Transparent speck glaze

Lead bisilicate (Ferro 3498)	80
Zinc oxide	10
China clay	5
Bentonite	5

A shiny, runny, slightly crystalline glaze with iron flecks.

---

6   Clear glaze

Lead bisilicate (Ferro 3498)	60
Standard borax frit (Ferro 3134)	35
Ball clay	5

A clear glaze with a slight crackle.

7   Transparent glaze

Calcium borate frit (Colemanite)	15
Lead bisilicate (Ferro 3498)	56
Ball clay	22
Flint	7

A clear, transparent glaze.

* * *

White, cream, opaque and matt glazes

8   Opaque milky white glaze

Standard borax frit (Ferro 3134)	80
Ball clay	10
Zirconium silicate	10

A smooth semi-opaque, milky white glaze.

Variation 1
With an addition of 3% cobalt oxide this glaze produces a rich dark blue colour.

Variation 2
With an addition of 4% copper oxide it gives a mottled grass green colour.

9   Semi-opaque white glaze

Standard borax frit (Ferro 3134)	65

Barium carbonate	15
Ball clay	10
Zirconium silicate	10

A smooth, semi-opaque, white glaze.

---

10 ✳ Opalescent blue white glaze

Calcium borate frit (Colemanite)	75
Feldspar	15
Ball clay	10

A clear glaze which runs blue-white opalescent where thick.

Variations
With the addition of 10% tin oxide, 4% iron oxide and 4% manganese oxide, this glaze gives a black, mottled cream, mushroom colour effect.

---

11   Shiny white glaze

Standard borax frit (Ferro 3134)	80
Ball clay	9
Zirconium silicate	11

A smooth, even, shiny white, opaque glaze.

---

12   Shiny cream tan glaze

Standard borax frit (Ferro 3134)	75
Ball clay	10

Zirconium silicate   15
Rutile   15%

A smooth, opaque, semi-shiny, cream tan coloured glaze.

---

13   Semi-opaque cream tan glaze

Calcium borate frit   8
(Colemanite)
Lead bisilicate   60
(Ferro 3498)
Feldspar   16
Flint   4
Bentonite   4
Rutile   8

A stiff, semi-opaque, cream tan glaze.

Variation
With the addition of 10% zirconium silicate and 3% cobalt oxide, a semi-matt, dark green glaze results.

---

14   Cream Vellum glaze

Lead bisilicate   78
(Ferro 3498)
Zinc oxide   4
Titanium dioxide   6
Ball clay   12

A cream, semi-matt, vellum surfaced glaze.

Variation
With the addition of 2% red iron oxide and 0.5% cobalt oxide, a semi-matt, black-brown glaze results.

15   Semi-opaque white stone glaze

Lead bisilicate (Ferro 3498)	40
Standard borax frit (Ferro 3134)	25
Whiting	20
China clay	10
Flint	5
Tin oxide	5%

A matt, semi-opaque white glaze, stone-like in quality.

16   White vellum glaze

Lead bisilicate (Ferro 3498)	80
Zinc oxide	3
China clay	17
Rutile	5%
Tin oxide	9%

A cream white, opaque vellum satin glaze.

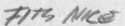

17   Smooth vellum glaze

Lead bisilicate (Ferro 3498)	80
Zinc oxide	3
Ball clay	17
Titanium dioxide	6%
Tin oxide	12%

A smooth, satin, cream white glaze which speckles well on a red body.

18   Milky white glaze

Lead bisilicate	70
(Ferro 3498)	
Feldspar	20
Whiting	6
China clay	4
Tin oxide	10%

A milky white, opaque glaze.

19   Soft white glaze

Lead bisilicate	80
(Ferro 3498)	
Zinc oxide	5
China clay	10
Flint	5
Tin oxide	12%

An even, semi-opaque, soft white glaze.

20   Satin matt glaze

Calcium borate frit	50
(Colemanite)	
Lithium carbonate	14
Barium carbonate	17
China clay	12
Flint	7

A satin matt glaze, semi-clear; apply thickly.

Variation
With addition of 15% iron oxide and 1% nickel oxide a matt black
glaze results.

* * *

Coloured and decorative glazes

21 Gold tan glaze

Lead bisilicate	74
(Ferro 3498)	
China clay	15
Rutile	11

A smooth, opaque, gold tan glaze. Apply thickly for a mottled effect.

Fits Nice

22 Opalescent blue glaze

Spodumene	20
Calcium borate frit	60
(Colemanite)	
Ball clay	12
Flint	8
Rutile	3%

An opalescent glaze, clear where thin, blue-white opalescent where thick.

Variation
The addition of 0.75% cobalt carbonate gives a rich, mottled, midnight blue glaze.

23 Dark grass green glaze

Lead bisilicate	60
(Ferro 3498)	
Feldspar (soda)	15
Cornish stone	12
Whiting	6
Zinc oxide	4

Flint	3
Nickel oxide	4%

A smooth, dark, grass green, opaque glaze. Do not apply too thickly.

---

24 ✳ Muted turquoise glaze

Standard borax frit (Ferro 3134)	55
Whiting	6
Ball clay	8
Zirconium silicate	18
Rutile (medium)	8
Copper carbonate	3
Cobalt oxide	2

A semi-shiny, opaque glaze, mottled dark turquoise in colour.

---

25 ✳ A mottled dark turquoise glaze

Standard borax frit (Ferro 3134)	75
Ball clay	15
Zirconium silicate	10
Copper carbonate	6%
Cobalt oxide	3%

A smooth, shiny, opaque glaze with a mottled, dark turquoise colour.

---

26 ✳ Mottled turquoise green glaze

Standard borax frit (Ferro 3134)	75
Ball clay	15

Zirconium silicate	10
Copper carbonate	5%

A smooth, opaque glaze, mottled turquoise green in colour.

---

27 ✳ Blue grey speckle glaze

Lead bisilicate (Ferro 3498)	35
Whiting	4
Standard borax frit (Ferro 3134)	25
Feldspar (soda)	18
Flint	5
Rutile	5
Zirconium silicate	8
Cobalt oxide	1%

A smooth, semi-opaque, blue grey speckle glaze.

---

28 ✳ Bright turquoise glaze

Standard borax frit (Ferro 3134)	50
Feldspar (soda)	35
Whiting	5
China clay	4
Flint	6
Copper oxide	1%

A smooth, turquoise green glaze. Apply thickly.

---

29 ✳ Bright turquoise blue glaze

Standard borax frit (Ferro 3134)	42

Calcium borate frit	22
(Colemanite)	
Whiting	7
Feldspar	20
Bentonite	5
Flint	4
Copper oxide	3%
Cobalt oxide	0.5%

A smooth, bright, mottled, turquoise blue glaze.

---

30   Opaque holly green glaze

Standard borax frit	90
(Ferro 3134)	
China clay	10
Chrome oxide	2%

A smooth, shiny, holly green glaze.

Variation
A further addition of 2% chrome oxide (total 4%) gives a more intense green colour.

---

31   Buttery yellow glaze

Calcium borate frit	50
(Colemanite)	
Whiting	10
Zinc oxide	15
Barium carbonate	3
China clay	14
Flint	3
Titanium dioxide	5

A shiny, opaque, butter yellow glaze.

32   Antique green glaze

Standard borax frit (Ferro 3134)	80
Zinc oxide	10
Ball clay	10
Zirconium silicate	10%
Ilmenite	10%
Copper carbonate	5%

A smooth, shiny, opaque, 'antique' green glaze.

33 ✳ Rich mottled black green glaze

Standard borax frit (Ferro 3134)	73
Barium carbonate	4
Ball clay	13
Zirconium silicate	10
Manganese carbonate	8%
Ilmenite	10%
Copper oxide	5%

A shiny, smooth, opaque glaze with a rich, mottled, black green colour.

Earthenware Glazes 1100 °C ~ 1150 °C (2012 °F ~ 2102 °F) Orton cones 03 ~ 01

Transparent glazes

---

34   **Clear glaze**

Calcium borate frit	50
(Colemanite)	
Whiting	6
Ball clay	16
China clay	16
Flint	12

A clear glaze: frothy, bubbled, semi-clear when fired at lower temperatures.

---

35   **Clear opalescent glaze**

Calcium borate frit	55
(Colemanite)	
Whiting	8
China clay	12
Red clay	15
Flint	10

A good clear, well-fitting glaze with a tendency to give slight opalescence where thick.

Variation
The addition of 2% red iron oxide gives a warmer, slightly honey-coloured glaze.

---

36   Clear glaze

Lead bisilicate	60
(Ferro 3498)	
Whiting	4
Feldspar	30
China clay	6

A clear, transparent glaze.

---

37   Clear glaze

Lead bisilicate	60
(Ferro 3498)	
Feldspar	10
Whiting	5
China clay	15
Flint	10

A clear, transparent glaze.

---

38   Semi-clear glaze

Lead bisilicate	60
(Ferro 3498)	
Standard borax frit	13
(Ferro 3134)	
Feldspar	10
China clay	12
Flint	5

A semi-clear glaze.

Variation
With the addition of 10% zirconium silicate and 3% copper carbonate
a bright grass green glaze results.

39	Clear glaze	
Lead bisilicate (Ferro 3498)		25
Standard borax frit (Ferro 3134)		50
Cornish stone		10
Ball clay		5
Flint		10

A clear glaze.

* * *

White, cream, opaque and matt glazes

40	Smooth cream glaze	
Standard borax frit (Ferro 3134)		70
China clay		20
Flint		10
Rutile (medium)		4%

A smooth, wide-firing, cream coloured, opaque glaze.

41	Muted cream tan glaze	
Standard borax frit (Ferro 3134)		70
Ball clay		15
Zirconium silicate		15

Rutile	5%
Red iron oxide	3%

A smooth, semi-matt, cream tan coloured, opaque glaze.

---

42   Stone white glaze

Lead bisilicate (Ferro 3498)	40
Standard borax frit (Ferro 3134)	25
Feldspar	14
Talc	12
Bentonite	3
Tin oxide	6

A matt, semi-opaque, cream white glaze.

---

43   Matt stone white glaze

Lead bisilicate (Ferro 3498)	50
Feldspar	25
Whiting	10
China clay	15
Titanium dioxide	3%
Tin oxide	8%

A stone-like, matt white glaze.

---

44   Creamy blue glaze

Calcium borate frit (Colemanite)	65

Red clay	25
Titanium dioxide	10

A smooth, semi-opaque, creamy glaze with blue grey mottling where thick, a rich iron tan where thin.

---

46   Semi-opaque glaze

Calcium borate frit (Colemanite)	45
Feldspar	35
Ball clay	15
Flint	5

A semi-opaque, shiny glaze which will clear at higher temperatures.

---

45   Creamy white semi-opaque glaze

Calcium borate frit (Colemanite)	75
Zinc oxide	13
Ball clay	12
Tin oxide	5%
Titanium dioxide	3%

A shiny, creamy white, semi-opaque glaze which breaks a bright tan on edges.

---

47   White opaque glaze

Calcium borate frit (Colemanite)	40

Ball clay	20
Flint	40

A semi-opaque, deep white glaze.

Variation 1
An addition of 4% tin oxide gives a more opaque bright white.

Variation 2
An addition of 0.75% cobalt oxide and 2% red iron oxide gives a speckled, blue grey, opaque effect.

* * *

Decorative and coloured glazes

48 ✳ Pink tan glaze

Standard borax frit (Ferro 3134)	70
Zinc oxide	6
Barium carbonate	2
China clay	10
Zirconium silicate	5
Rutile	5
Manganese carbonate	2

An opaque, pink tan, shiny glaze.

49   Clear base glaze

Lead bisilicate (Ferro 3498)	65
Whiting	5
Ball clay	10

| China clay | 10 |
| Flint | 10 |

A clear base glaze.

Variation
With the addition of 5% rutile, 0.5% chrome oxide, 0.5% cobalt oxide and 5% red iron oxide, it gives a smooth black brown colour.

---

50 ✬ Pale green lava glaze

Standard borax frit	60
(Ferro 3134)	
Zinc oxide	20
China clay	5
Flint	5
Rutile (medium)	10
Silicon carbide	0.5%
Copper oxide	1%

A decorative lava glaze with a bubbled surface. Do not apply too thickly.

---

51 ✬ Brown oil glaze

Standard borax frit	92
(Ferro 3134)	
China clay	8
Red iron oxide	15%

A dark 'oil' black brown glaze. Do not apply too thickly.

---

52 ✳ Pale green lava textured glaze

Standard borax frit	60
(Ferro 3134)	
Zinc oxide	20

China clay	5
Flint	5
Rutile (medium)	10
Silicon carbide	0.5%
Nickel oxide	2%

A lava textured, decorative glaze, pale green in colour.

---

53 ✳ Grey/pink/green glaze

Standard borax frit (Ferro 3134)	65
Ball clay	8
Zirconium silicate	20
Iron oxide	7

A smooth, opaque muted grey/pink/green glaze.

Medium Temperature Stoneware Glazes 1200 °C ~ 1220 °C (2192 °F ~ 2228 °F) Orton cone 5

Transparent and semi-transparent glazes

---

54   Good transparent glaze

Feldspar	40
Calcium borate frit	35
(Colemanite)	
Ball clay	15
Flint	10

A clear, well fitting glaze.

---

55   Clear glaze

Feldspar (soda)	40
Calcium borate frit	30
(Colemanite)	
Ball clay	20
Flint	10

A clear, transparent glaze.

56   Clear transparent glaze

Lithium carbonate	5
Whiting	15
Standard borax frit	15
(Ferro 3134)	
China clay	30
Flint	35

A basic, clear glaze with a slight blue cast.

57   Semi-transparent ash glaze

Feldspar	12
Wood ash	42
Calcium borate frit	32
(Colemanite)	
Ball clay	14

A runny, semi-transparent, broken ash glaze; more broken over dark clay or slips.

58   Semi-transparent ash glaze

Feldspar	20
Alkaline leadless frit	30
(Ferro 3110)	
Wood ash	40
Ball clay	10

A semi-transparent, slightly crazed, glaze.

59   Transparent glaze

Zinc oxide	5
Whiting	10

Cryolite	20
Ball clay	15
Flint	50

A semi-matt, transparent glaze, with a pale blue cast over a dark body or slip.

---

60   Transparent, semi-matt glaze

Calcium borate frit (Colemanite)	45
Ball clay	12
China clay	13
Flint	30

A clear glaze with a slightly bubbly quality.

---

61   Semi-transparent glaze

Alkaline leadless frit (Ferro 3110)	45
Lithium carbonate	5
Whiting	15
Ball clay	10
Flint	25

A shiny glaze with pale blue chun streaks where thick.

Variation
An addition of 3% manganese carbonate gives a slightly mauve coloured glaze.

---

62   Clear transparent glaze

Feldspar	15
Calcium borate frit	15

(Colemanite)
Petalite   14
Dolomite   20
Ball clay   16
Flint   20

A clear and transparent glaze, slightly opaque, with white streaks when thick.

---

63   Transparent glaze

Nepheline syenite   40
Whiting   15
Zinc oxide   10
Ball clay   5
Flint   30

A clear, transparent glaze with a tendency to move over the clay surface.

Variation
With an addition of 2% red iron oxide, it gives a pale honey colour.

---

64   Stiff transparent glaze

Nepheline syenite   30
Dolomite   10
Zinc oxide   5
Calcium borate frit   10
(Colemanite)
Ball clay   10
Flint   35

A clear, transparent, stiff glaze. If applied thickly it will collect air bubbles. Good over both light and dark clay bodies.

65 ✳ Clear transparent glaze

Nepheline syenite	40
Wollastonite	15
Zinc oxide	12
Ball clay	5
Flint	28

A clear, transparent glaze; where thicker, it tends to froth and go slightly opaque.

✳ Variation

A brown oil spot glaze can be formed by the addition of the following oxides: iron oxide 2%, manganese oxide 2%, cobalt oxide 1%, chromium oxide 1%. With these oxide additions, it has a dark brown mirror-like effect, with 'oil-spot' speckles over a darker body.

66   Transparent glaze

Nepheline syenite	45
Whiting	3
Calcium borate frit (Colemanite)	20
Barium carbonate	10
Flint	22

A clear, transparent glaze with a tendency to craze.

67   Speckled transparent glaze

Nepheline syenite	15
Calcium borate frit (Colemanite)	50
China clay	17
Flint	18
Rutile	5%

A bright transparent glaze with iron speckles. It will give a blue chun effect over a dark clay body.

68 ✳ Chun glaze

Feldspar	45
Whiting	5
Calcium borate frit	20
(Colemanite)	
Flint	30

A chun effect glaze caused by trapped air bubbles in the glaze, giving a soft pale blue colour. It will especially give a blue over a dark clay body.

* * *

White, cream, matt, opaque glazes

69 ✳ White matt opaque glaze

Nepheline syenite	45
Calcium borate frit	10
(Colemanite)	
Barium carbonate	15
Wollastonite	15
Ball clay	10
Flint	5
Tin oxide	8%

A matt, opaque white glaze. When thick, it goes slightly pink on a light coloured body. It has an attractive speckle white/grey colour over a dark coloured body or slip.

70   Silky white glaze

Feldspar (soda)	45
Whiting	20

Zinc oxide	10
China clay	20
Flint	5

A smooth, semi-matt, silky white glaze, slightly pinholed and more opaque over a red body.

---

71 ✳ Speckled cream white/pink glaze — *NICE MATT GLAZE TIB. RED LITTLE SOMBER. AT 46*

Feldspar *POT – KALI*	25
Barium carbonate	10
Zinc oxide	5
Whiting	20
Spodumene	20
Ball clay	8
Flint	12

An opaque, semi-matt, crystal surfaced, slightly runny glaze.

Variation 1
With an addition of 8% tin oxide, it gives a matt, stone-like, speckle glaze, slightly runny; this goes very slightly pink in thick areas.

Variation 2
With an addition of 8% tin oxide and 0.5% chromium oxide, it produces a matt, opaque, broken and mottled pink glaze, slightly orange on a darker body.

---

72   White dolomite glaze

Dolomite	40
Lepidolite	50
Flint	10
Bentonite	3%

A matt surfaced, white, opaque glaze, giving a typical dolomite effect. It has a tendency to run if overfired, and stains slightly yellow over a dark iron body.

73   Vellum glaze

Nepheline syenite	20
Zinc oxide	20
Whiting	10
Ball clay	20
Talc	30
Titanium dioxide	10%

A pale, semi-matt surface, with a vellum-like finish. Good over both dark and light clay bodies.

74   Frosty white glaze

Nepheline syenite	42
Whiting	10
Zinc oxide	18
Flint	30
Bentonite	3%

A frosty white glaze with crystal formation where thick, clear where thin. It gives a better effect over a lighter coloured body.

75   Semi-opaque white glaze

Cryolite	25
Fluorspar	15
Ball clay	20
Flint	40

This glaze is frosty white when thick; slightly yellow over a dark coloured body or slip.

76   Matt opaque orange-white

Cornish stone	30
Petalite	30
Calcium borate frit	10
(Colemanite)	
Talc	20
Zinc oxide	3
Cryolite	2
Bentonite	5
Tin oxide	4%

A speckled, white-orange, matt glaze with a smooth surface and a pleasant semi-matt finish.

77   Smooth matt opaque glaze

Nepheline syenite	45
Calcium borate frit	5
(Colemanite)	
Whiting	5
Dolomite	15
Ball clay	20
Flint	10

A smooth surfaced, white, semi-opaque glaze.

78   Dry ash glaze

Nepheline syenite	30
Dolomite	15
Wood ash	35
Ball clay	20

A dry, semi-opaque, matt white glaze. Apply thickly.

79   White fat glaze

Nepheline syenite	40
Alkaline frit	10
(Ferro 3110)	
Whiting	15
Ball clay	5
Flint	30

An opaque white, semi-matt glaze with a fat surface quality. Apply thickly to the pot.

80   Frosty matt glaze

Nepheline syenite	50
Lead bisilicate	30
(Ferro 3498)	
Whiting	20
Bentonite	3%

A decorative glaze with speckles and orange spots. It is slightly runny; do not overfire. This glaze can be coloured with oxide additions.

81   Dry stone glaze

Nepheline syenite	47
Whiting	7
Dolomite	16
Lead bisilicate	8
(Ferro 3498)	
Ball clay	22

A dry, matt-white, opaque stone glaze.

82   White stone glaze

Feldspar	50
Whiting	5
Dolomite	15
Lead bisilicate	10
(Ferro 3498)	
China clay	20

A very dry, white, opaque, matt glaze.

83   Cream stone glaze

Nepheline syenite	25
Calcium borate frit	5
(Colemanite)	
Wollastonite	25
Red clay	20
Ball clay	25

A dry stone-like glaze, opaque and matt.

Variation
With an addition of 2% red iron oxide and 3% rutile, a mottled cream-brown glaze results.

84   Broken white glaze

Feldspar	40
Standard borax frit	25
(Ferro 3134)	
Dolomite	10
Fluorspar	10
China clay	15

A frosty, semi-transparent glaze with a cream colour, best over a dark coloured clay or slip.

85   Pale blue/white matt glaze

Feldspar	40
Whiting	20
Dolomite	5
Barium Carbonate	15
Ball clay	10
Flint	10

A matt, opaque, pale blue/white glaze.

86   Semi-dry white glaze

Cornish stone	13
Feldspar	40
Whiting	23
Zinc oxide	7
Ball clay	10
China clay	7

A rich, semi-matt, white glaze.

87   White opaque glaze

Feldspar	22
Flint	17
Dolomite	3
Calcium borate frit (Colemanite)	36
Ball clay	22
Tin oxide	6%

A white, opaque glaze with iron speckles, which breaks on edges to show the body.

88   Frosty white glaze

Nepheline syenite	40
Wollastonite	15
Barium carbonate	25
Red clay	15
Flint	5

Suitable for a light coloured body, this matt, frosty white glaze is broken when thick.

Variation
An addition of 1% copper carbonate gives an attractive turquoise colour.

89   Shiny opaque white glaze

Feldspar	50
Whiting	5
Lithium carbonate	5
Zinc oxide	12
Ball clay	15
Flint	13

Typical shiny, opaque, white zinc glaze with slight crystal formations.

90   Honey-cream matt glaze

Nepheline syenite	30
Whiting	10
Zinc oxide	10
Red clay	40
Flint	10

A pale honey cream, opaque, stable glaze, good over light and dark coloured bodies.

91   Pale cream matt glaze

Lithium carbonate	10
Talc	10
Whiting	10
Ball clay	25
Flint	45

A smooth, semi-opaque, semi-matt, cream coloured glaze, with a mottled effect over a dark body or slip. It loses colour if applied too thinly.

92   Semi-opaque white glaze

Feldspar	30
Dolomite	10
Lithium carbonate	5
Whiting	10
Ball clay	10
Flint	35

A semi-opaque, matt, white glaze, attractive on a dark body or over slips.

Variation
With the addition of 8% red iron oxide, it gives a shiny glaze, dark brown with light mustard coloured crystals.

93   Matt yellow/cream glaze

Lithium carbonate	10
Whiting	10
Dolomite	15
Ball clay	25
Flint	40

A semi-opaque, matt, yellow/cream glaze: bright over a cream body, darker mottled beige over a red body.

94   Dry stone glaze

Feldspar	45
Whiting	7
Barium carbonate	10
Zinc oxide	6
Talc	4
Ball clay	5
China clay	5
Flint	18
Nickel oxide	2%

A glaze with a dry, stone-like effect. Pale off-white; better on darker clay or over slips.

95   Speckled beige glaze

Cornish stone	18
Feldspar	35
Zinc oxide	6
Whiting	23
Ball clay	10
China clay	8

Semi-matt, streaky beige/brown glaze. More attractive over a lighter body; darker yellow over a red body.

96   Opaque 'mutton fat' glaze

Feldspar	48
Whiting	7
Ball clay	5
Flint	20
Barium carbonate	20

A smooth, opaque, white glaze with a distinct crackle resembling old Chinese glazes. A thick application is essential. It goes clear at higher temperatures.

97   Oatmeal speckle glaze

Feldspar	35
Cornish stone	15
Zinc oxide	6
Whiting	30
Ball clay	14

A speckled, oatmeal effect; this glaze is slightly runny where thick. It gives a dryer effect over a dark body.

* * *

Coloured, decorative and crystal glazes

98   Broken pearl glaze

Feldspar	28
Whiting	14
Dolomite	14
Zinc oxide	10
Lithium carbonate	3
Bentonite	4
Flint	20
Rutile	7

A decorative, pale blue-grey, streaky pearl glaze; do not overfire.

99   Frosty matt rust glaze

Lithium carbonate	10
Whiting	50

1 *Above* Porcelain cast goblets by Gwyneth Newland, with sprayed glaze 221 with (left and right) an addition of 1.5 copper oxide and (centre) 4% tin oxide

2 *Below* Porcelain bowl, oxidized, with glaze 381 including an addition of 2% nickel oxide: this gives a smooth satin surface with rich pale green and brown mottled patterns

3 An example of an overfired body. A rich green brown glaze was used on a stoneware body, oxidized; the quality of the runny glaze can be seen, but overfiring caused the body to bloat. (Glaze: Fremington clay 70, whiting 20, flint 10)

4 Porcelain bowl, fired in a reduction kiln, with a crawled glaze caused by putting the pot into a hot kiln before the glaze had properly dried; this dried out the glaze too quickly, and it flaked off the pot and subsequently crawled into lumps during the firing

5 Stoneware pot with glaze 231, variation 3, using 1% copper carbonate: this gives a pale green effect with cream coloured crystals

6 Stoneware cup, oxidized, glaze 410, with 'clotted blood red' variation:
the bottom colour is a rich maroon red, and the glaze tends to run clear
on the rim

7 Round pot and lid with glaze 404, oxidized, resulting in a bright shocking pink with blue areas when the glaze is thinner

8 Oval pot and lid with glaze 71, variation 2, oxidized, resulting in a
bright crimson pink from the 0.5% chromium oxide; fired to 1220°C
(2228°F)

9 Porcelain bowl, oxidized, with glaze 148 plus 2% manganese oxide; a pale pink-blue glaze with delicate markings, sometimes resembling an iridescent oil slick, this glaze heightens and picks out incised decoration

10 *Above* A semi-clear glaze (221 with 5% uranium oxide) with fine craze lines on a porcelain bowl, oxidized, fired to 1260°C (2300°F)
11 *Below* A typical crackle effect in a matt opaque glaze with 1.5% copper carbonate on a porcelain bowl, oxidized, fired to 1260°C (2300°F)

12 A mottled matt effect with smooth crystalline formation in a glaze
which contains titanium and copper, oxidized, fired to 1260°C
(2300°F)

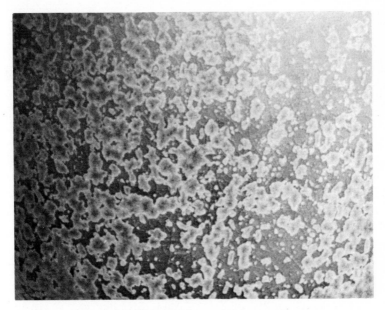

13 A 'sea froth' effect of pale green crystals in a darker green background, produced by glaze 380, variation 2, oxidized

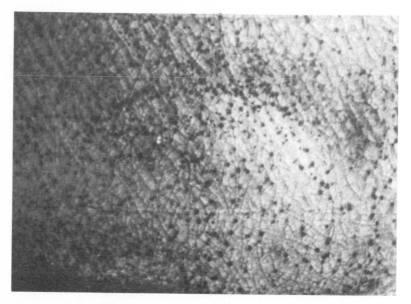

14 A 'cobra skin' effect produced by glaze 221 plus 2% copper oxide, oxidized, on porcelain; this gives a rich green glaze with pale yellow and black crystal formations when applied thickly, and a matt black when thin

15 Glaze 36, a semi-clear earthenware glaze fired to 1060°C (1940°F) which traps air bubbles when thickly applied; a higher temperature is required to 'clear' the glaze

16 Glaze 25, a shiny, opaque, mottled blue-green glaze with dark blue flecks fired to 1060°C (1940°F)

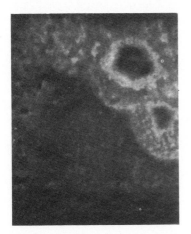

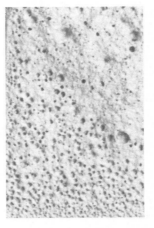

17 Glaze 10, variation, a mottled semi-matt cream-brown glaze, lighter in colour when applied more thickly, fired to 1060°C (1940°F)

18 Glaze 50, a decorative 'lava' effect glaze, fired to 1060°C (1940°F)

19 Glaze 446, smooth matt with dark pink red crystal formations in a green coloured background, oxidized, fired to 1260°C (2300°F)

20 Glaze 416, a semi-smooth glaze with silver green crystals, oxidized, fired to 1260°C (2300°F)

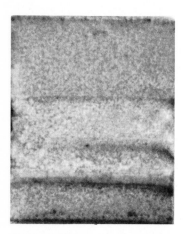

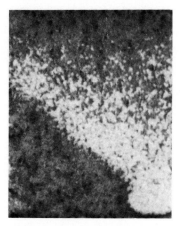

21 Glaze 440, a yellow cream matt glaze, fired to 1260°C (2300°F)

22 Glaze 218, a clear glaze with a white frothy crystal formation when applied thickly, fired to 1260°C (2300°F)

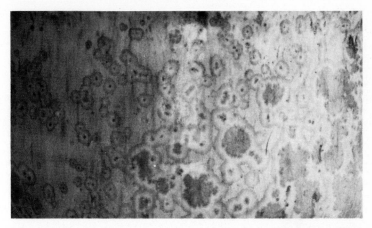

23 Zinc-silicate crystals in a stoneware glaze, oxidized, fired to 1260°C (2300°F)

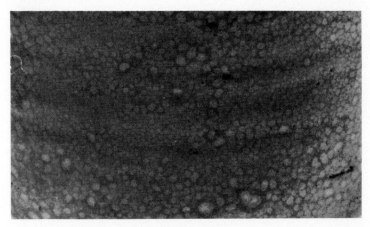

24 Stoneware oil-spot glaze effect, oxidized, fired to 1260°C (2300°F)

25 Stoneware pot with glaze 380, variation 2: a dark green glaze with lighter green crystal formations

Barium carbonate	35
Bentonite	5
Copper oxide	1%

A matt, frosty, decorative glaze with a rust coloured mottled effect.

FIRED CONE 6 AND DRIPPED UGLY

100 Runny pink-purple glaze

Nepheline syenite	25
Barium carbonate	37
Lithium carbonate	5
Zinc oxide	12
Flint	18
Bentonite	3
Nickel oxide	1.5%

This is suitable for use only on a light coloured body to give a runny, purple-pink glaze; do not overfire.

101 Crystalline glaze

Nepheline syenite	20
Lithium carbonate	8
Whiting	6
Zinc oxide	20
Ball clay	3
Flint	35
Titanium dioxide	8
Copper oxide	1.5%
Nickel oxide	1%
Cobalt oxide	0.5%

A light cream coloured glaze with white-pink crystal growths.

102   Ash glaze

Wood ash	40
Alkaline frit	40
(Ferro 3110)	
Ball clay	20

A semi-transparent, runny glaze over a light coloured clay. A more interesting broken glaze over dark clay or slip.

103   Brown, blue spotted glaze

Barium carbonate	40
Zinc oxide	12
Alkaline frit	30
(Ferro 3110)	
Lithium carbonate	2
Ball clay	10
Flint	6
Nickel oxide	1.5%

A runny, matt glaze with bright blue areas when thick; colours shown only on light coloured areas.

Variation
With 1.5% copper carbonate instead of nickel oxide a runny pale green and pale brown glaze results.

104   Broken blue/yellow glaze

Feldspar	23
Nepheline syenite	10
Calcium borate frit	8
(Colemanite)	
Barium carbonate	10
Zinc oxide	20
Talc	12

| Ball clay | 7 |
| Flint | 10 |

A runny, matt surfaced, semi-opaque glaze, which goes pale blue when thick. It has a pleasant satin surface, and stains pale yellow over a dark coloured body.

---

105   Mottled blue-yellow glaze

Nepheline syenite	30
Whiting	10
Lithium carbonate	5
Calcium borate frit	15
(Colemanite)	
Talc	5
Barium carbonate	10
Ball clay	5
Flint	20
Cobalt oxide	0.5%
Red iron oxide	2%

A mottled blue glaze which goes yellow where thin.

---

106   Mauve-green glaze

Feldspar	45
Barium carbonate	30
Zinc oxide	7
Flint	15
Bentonite	3
Nickel oxide	1.5%

A shiny, runny glaze which goes mauve/purple where thin, and dark green-purple where thick.

107✗ Pale purple glaze

Feldspar	35
Barium carbonate	35
Lithium carbonate	3
Zinc oxide	3
Talc	4
Ball clay	5
Flint	15
Nickel oxide	1.5%

Suitable for use only on a light coloured body, to give a smooth, matt, opaque, pale purple glaze.

Variation
With 2% copper carbonate replacing the nickel oxide a rich turquoise colour results.

108   Clear grass green glaze

Nepheline syenite	15
Standard borax frit (Ferro 3134)	20
Whiting	10
Talc	5
Barium carbonate	10
Flint	40
Chromium oxide	0.5%

A cool, shiny, clear, grass green glaze; bright and luminous over porcelain, muted on stoneware. Stable at higher temperatures.

109   White bubble glaze

Feldspar	55
Lithium carbonate	10

Whiting	10
Ball clay	5
Flint	20

A decorative white-blue glaze which gives an attractive sparkly effect.

---

110   Pink/blue glaze

Feldspar	50
Whiting	8
Zinc oxide	10
Barium carbonate	20
Ball clay	6
Flint	6
Nickel oxide	1%

A rich but subtle pale blue/pink, matt, opaque glaze.

---

111   Yellow slip glaze

Zinc oxide	20
Fremington clay	80
(Albany slip)	

A pale mustard-brown glaze.

Variation
Additions of black iron oxide will give a darker colour.

---

112   Streaky green glaze

Nepheline syenite	35
Whiting	26
Calcium borate frit	6
(Colemanite)	

Dolomite	6
Zinc oxide	3
Barium carbonate	4
China clay	5
Flint	15
Tin oxide	3%
Copper carbonate	2%

A runny, streaky glaze, pleasantly mottled on stoneware, a rich green on a porcelain body. Do not overfire.

* * *

Base glazes for oxide additions

113   Turquoise glaze base

Nepheline syenite	30
Whiting	5
Zinc oxide	5
Barium carbonate	30
Ball clay	10
Flint	20

Variation 1
With 1% of copper carbonate a very pale turquoise glaze is obtained; 2% gives a stronger and richer effect. Not suitable for use on dark bodies.

Variation 2
An addition of 0.5% cobalt carbonate gives a matt, opaque, medium cobalt blue colour.

114   Frosty white speckle glaze base

Nepheline syenite	60
Standard borax frit	20
(Ferro 3134)	

Whiting	18
Bentonite	2

A frosty, semi-opaque glaze with iron speckles. It has a tendency to go transparent when thick and is iron yellow over a dark coloured body.

Variation 1
With 2% copper carbonate the glaze goes pale green with dark green runs; black where thin.

Variation 2
With the addition of 1% cobalt oxide and 2% red iron oxide a streaky glaze results, with shiny and matt runs in blue, yellow and black.

---

115   Crystal milky glaze base

Feldspar	52
Whiting	12
Zinc oxide	9
Barium carbonate	22
Bentonite	5

A milky white glaze, slightly runny to give an interesting semi-opaque variation.

Variation 1
With additions of 2% dark rutile, 4% manganese carbonate and 5% borax frit, a stone purple glaze results.

Variation 2
With an addition of 2% dark rutile and 2% nickel oxide a speckled green/yellow/orange glaze results.

---

116   Clear transparent glaze base

Standard borax frit	40
(Ferro 3134)	
Cryolite	2
Calcium borate frit	4
(Colemanite)	

Ball clay	30
Flint	24

A clear, transparent, semi-matt glaze.

Variation 1
With an addition of 6% tin oxide a shiny white opaque glaze results.

Variation 2
With the addition of 5% tin oxide and 1.5% copper carbonate an opaque pale speckled green glaze results.

Variation 3
An addition of 5% tin oxide and 3% iron oxide gives a shiny opaque brown-orange glaze.

Variation 4
An addition of 5% tin oxide, 2% iron oxide and 0.5% cobalt carbonate gives a speckled opaque grey blue glaze.

---

117   Frosty glaze base

Nepheline syenite	50
Barium carbonate	30
Standard borax frit	10
(Ferro 3134)	
Lithium carbonate	5
Bentonite	5

A frosty, matt glaze, even and semi-opaque, suitable for use on light and medium coloured bodies.

Variation 1
With an addition of 2% copper carbonate, a rich blue turquoise colour results.

Variation 2
With an addition of 4% tin oxide and 2% copper carbonate a pale, even, blue turquoise glaze results.

Variation 3
With an addition of 0.5% cobalt carbonate a rich blue-purple glaze results.

118   Matt smooth glaze base

Alkaline frit	28
(Ferro 3110)	
Whiting	4
Dolomite	15
Lithium carbonate	5
Ball clay	18
Flint	30

The base glaze is semi-opaque white with a mottled effect over a dark body or slip.

Variation 1
With an addition of 1% chromium oxide a green/grey glaze results.

Variation 2
With an addition of 0.5% cobalt oxide and 1% chromium oxide a more opaque, holly-green glaze results.

Variation 3
With the addition of 2% iron oxide and 0.5% cobalt oxide a mottled mustard olive brown glaze results.

119   Broken glaze base

Nepheline syenite	50
Whiting	20
Standard borax frit	26
(Ferro 3134)	
Bentonite	4

A speckled, semi-opaque, matt glaze, which breaks attractively.

Variation 1
With an addition of 1% copper carbonate a mottled pale green grey glaze results.

Variaton 2
An addition of 4% rutile and 0.5% cobalt oxide gives a mottled pale blue mauve glaze.

120   Semi-dry glaze base

Feldspar	30
Nepheline syenite	12
Calcium borate frit	10
(Colemanite)	
Barium carbonate	10
Zinc oxide	20
Ball clay	5
Flint	13

A dry, frosty glaze with few highlights.

Variation 1
With an addition of 0.5% nickel oxide a dry, opaque, midnight blue glaze results.

Variation 2
An addition of 4% rutile gives a mottle white, clear glaze.

121   White crystal glaze base

Alkaline frit	40
(Ferro 3110)	
Zinc oxide	25
Bentonite	4
Flint	25
Titanium dioxide	6

A clear glaze with white and cream crystal formations on porcelain. On stoneware it gives a mottled orange white. Do not overfire.

Variation
Different oxides will give a wide range of colouring effects.

122   Crystal glaze base

Zinc oxide	20
Lithium carbonate	10

Titanium dioxide	8
Whiting	5
Ball clay	20
Flint	37

A pale cream, semi-matt, opaque glaze with pale pink crystal growths.

Variation
With the addition of 1% nickel oxide a pale cream yellow glaze results.

* * *

Brown and black iron glazes — olive to black

123   Brown/black 'hare's fur' glaze

Standard borax frit	85
(Ferro 3134)	
China clay	15
Red iron oxide	10%

A shiny, brown, 'hare's fur' effect glaze, good over light and dark bodies.

124   Brown adventurine glaze

Standard borax frit	76
(Ferro 3134)	
China clay	4
Bentonite	4
Red iron oxide	15
Copper carbonate	1

A shiny, speckled, dark brown adventurine glaze, which appears black on thin areas. It is good on both light and dark bodies.

125   Dry dark stone glaze

Nepheline syenite	20
Wollastonite	20
Red clay	35
Ball clay	25
Cobalt oxide	1%

A dark blue/grey glaze with a very dry, mottled effect; best when applied thickly.

126   Matt black slip glaze

Red clay	75
Manganese carbonate	25

A mottled, matt black, dry slip glaze.

127   Matt dry black-brown glaze

Nepheline syenite	30
Wollastonite	20
Barium carbonate	15
Red clay	25
Flint	10
Red iron oxide	3%
Cobalt oxide	2%
Manganese oxide	3%

A dry, matt, dark brown glaze with black speckles.

128   Orange skin dark matt glaze

Nepheline syenite	20
Wollastonite	20

Red clay	35
Ball clay	25
Iron oxide	2%
Cobalt oxide	1%
Manganese oxide	2%

A slip glaze, mottled brown, with dark speckles, dry and matt.

---

129   **Dark honey glaze**

Nepheline syenite	15
Whiting	10
Lithium carbonate	5
Red clay	35
Flint	35
Iron oxide	2%

A medium coloured, dark olive glaze.

Variation
With an addition of 2% manganese oxide a darker, broken brown glaze results.

---

130   **Dark honey glaze**

Volcanic ash	80
Whiting	10
Zinc oxide	10
Iron oxide	2%

A shiny, smooth, honey coloured glaze.

131   Pale honey glaze

Volcanic ash	65
Calcium borate frit	30
(Colemanite)	
Ball clay	5

A rich, pale honey coloured, transparent glaze.

132   Gold-brown matt glaze

Feldspar	28
Whiting	14
Zinc oxide	10
Lithium carbonate	3
Barium carbonate	3
Dolomite	12
Cryolite	7
Bentonite	5
Flint	18
Black iron oxide	10%
Rutile	6%

A matt, opaque glaze, which breaks a bright gold tan, and runs a darker brown. It has a tendency to run.

133   Metallic black glaze

Feldspar	36
Whiting	9
Calcium borate frit	5
(Colemanite)	
Dolomite	5
Talc	16

Barium carbonate	8
Flint	16
Bentonite	5
Zirconium silicate	15%
Rutile	20%
Cobalt oxide	3%
Manganese oxide	2%
Black iron oxide	3%

A matt, slightly crystalline, black glaze with a metallic surface.

134   Runny brown/yellow glaze

Feldspar	40
Cornish stone	13
Whiting	23
Zinc oxide	7
Ball clay	10
China clay	7
Black iron oxide	5%

A mottled, brown/yellow, semi-matt glaze.

135   Mottled brown/orange glaze

Alkaline frit	30
(Ferro 3110)	
Dolomite	15
Whiting	3
Lithium carbonate	3
Ball clay	30
Flint	19
Red iron oxide	7%

A broken brown glaze, runny, with a good colour over a lighter coloured body.

Stoneware Glazes with a Wide Firing Range 1200 °C ~ 1260 °C (2192 °F ~ 2300 °F) Orton cones 5, 6, 7 and 8

Transparent and semi-transparent glazes

---

136   White clear speckle glaze

Nepheline syenite	50
Whiting	5
Petalite	10
Dolomite	15
Zinc oxide	5
Zirconium silicate	15

A semi-clear glaze with white speckles in oxidation. In reduction it gives a pale speckled blue on porcelain, more yellow on stoneware. Do not overfire.

---

137   Stiff clear glaze

Cornish stone	40
Whiting	14
Dolomite	5
Zinc oxide	1
Ball clay	14
Flint	26

A stiff, clear, smooth, transparent glaze with slight bubbles in oxidation, pale blue green in reduction.

Variation 1
An addition of 5% red iron oxide gives a non-craze, smooth, transparent, rich honey glaze in oxidation, a dark green brown in reduction.

Variation 2
An addition of 8.5% red iron oxide gives a smooth red black glaze in oxidation, a rich black brown in reduction.

---

138   Clear glaze

Nepheline syenite	36
Calcium borate frit	7
(Colemanite)	
Dolomite	10
Zinc oxide	3
Barium carbonate	7
Bentonite	3
Flint	34
Tin oxide	1%
Red iron oxide	1%

A clear transparent glaze in oxidation, smooth and even over a wide temperature range. In reduction it gives a pale green on stoneware, a delicate 'baby blue' on porcelain.

---

139   Clear glaze

Feldspar	40
Whiting	15
Zinc oxide	10
Ball clay	5
China clay	10
Flint	20

Clear with tiny bubbles in a transparent glaze in oxidation; pale blue in reduction.

140   Smooth transparent glaze

Feldspar	30
Calcium borate frit (Colemanite)	10
Whiting	10
Barium carbonate	10
Ball clay	10
Flint	30

A clear, transparent glaze, slightly blue in reduction.

141   Chun clear glaze

Feldspar	50
Zinc oxide	4
Dolomite	10
Whiting	10
Bentonite	3
Flint	23

In oxidation a clear glaze with a chun translucent blue, especially at lower temperatures. In reduction a semi-clear, blue-grey glaze.

142   Clear glaze

Feldspar	50
Whiting	10
Dolomite	5
Zinc oxide	3
Ball clay	12
Flint	20

In oxidation a clear, slightly crazed glaze. In reduction a clear, pale blue grey glaze.

143   Clear glaze

Feldspar	60
Nepheline syenite	15
Zinc oxide	10
Whiting	10
Bentonite	5

In oxidation on porcelain a clear crazed glaze; slightly less smooth on stoneware. In reduction a pale, semi-clear, cool grey blue glaze.

144   Bright clear glaze

Petalite	60
Whiting	5
Barium carbonate	10
Calcium borate frit (Colemanite)	10
Ball clay	5
Flint	10

In oxidation a bright clear glaze, slightly speckled on stoneware. In reduction a semi-clear glaze with a slight matt effect.

145   Wide-firing transparent glaze

Feldspar	30
Zinc oxide	4
Whiting	15
Talc	3
Barium carbonate	10
China clay	10
Flint	28

A wide-firing clear glaze. At a lower temperature range a slight bubbly clear glaze results.

Variation
With the addition of 3% red iron oxide a pale honey glaze results in oxidation, a shiny pale green in oxidation.

---

146   Clear crackle glaze

Cornish stone *KALI VELD*	80	*POTASH*
Whiting	16	
Bentonite	4	

In oxidation, a clear transparent glaze with a distinctive crackle, especially on stoneware. In reduction, a clear transparent blue/grey colour on stoneware, pale blue on porcelain.

---

147   Watery clear glaze

Feldspar (soda)	40
Whiting	20
Ball clay	8
China clay	5
Flint	27

In oxidation a clear, transparent glaze with a slight crackle, better at a lower temperature range. In reduction a pale transparent green.

✳ 148   Wide-firing clear base glaze

Feldspar (soda)	38
Whiting	14
Zinc oxide	12
Ball clay	6
Flint	30

A semi-clear 'chun' glaze. In oxidation a semi-translucent, delicate 'chun' glaze, more clear in reduction.

Variation 1
With an addition of 1.5% copper oxide a translucent turquoise colour
develops in oxidation; in reduction a delicate mottled blood red colour.

Variation 2
With an addition of 2% manganese carbonate a translucent, iridescent
blue-pink develops in oxidation; in reduction a clear grey-green.

* * *

White, cream, matt, opaque glazes

---

149   Fine white speckle glaze

Nepheline syenite	35
Dolomite	15
Whiting	4
Zinc oxide	3
Ball clay	8
Flint	35

In oxidation semi-transparent white frosty speckle glaze, best over
porcelain. In reduction a cool, grey, speckle glaze over stoneware,
a pale blue over porcelain.

---

150   Matt smooth white glaze

Nepheline syenite	35
Dolomite	20
Whiting	5
China clay	20
Flint	20

In oxidation a dry, white, semi-opaque, matt glaze, deep white on
porcelain. In reduction a pale blue, matt glaze on porcelain, and iron
speckle on stoneware.

151   Pale cream green glaze

Nepheline syenite	29
Dolomite	30
Whiting	5
Zinc oxide	6
China clay	30

Best in reduction when a smooth, opaque glaze is obtained; pale green on stoneware, pale cream on porcelain. In oxidation it gives a matt, dry glaze.

152   White orange ash glaze

Nepheline syenite	55
Dolomite	18
Wood ash	10
Ball clay	5
Bentonite	2
Tin oxide	10

A white, opaque glaze, breaking orange on edges and where thin in oxidation. Pale, clear, yellow green in reduction; on stoneware speckled, on porcelain crazed, pale green. Do not overfire.

153   White matt glaze

Nepheline syenite	63
Whiting	10
Dolomite	5
Barium carbonate	10
China clay	10
Flint	2

In oxidation a snowy, stony white, matt glaze on stoneware, smoother on porcelain; in reduction a smooth opaque glaze. Do not overfire.

154   Tin white glaze

Feldspar	50
Whiting	5
Dolomite	25
China clay	20
Tin oxide	10%

A snowy white glaze on porcelain, slightly broken orange on stoneware in oxidation. In reduction it is a pale green on porcelain, a speckled opaque on stoneware.

155   White matt glaze

Nepheline syenite	40
Whiting	10
Dolomite	12
Zinc oxide	3
China clay	20
Flint	10
Zirconium oxide	5

In oxidation an opaque stone-like speckle matt glaze. In reduction a smooth matt glaze on porcelain, an iron speckle matt on stoneware.

156   White-yellow stone glaze

Nepheline syenite	60
Whiting	10
Dolomite	5
Barium carbonate	10
China clay	10
Flint	5

A stone glaze with a rich decorative surface, especially over a stoneware body. On porcelain a stony white, slightly pinholed glaze results in oxidation; more blue and satin-like in reduction.

157   Shiny white/blue speckle glaze

Nepheline syenite	58
Dolomite	18
Whiting	7
Zinc oxide	7
Petalite	10
Zirconium silicate	15%

A speckled white blue glaze in reduction or cream white in oxidation.
Do not overfire.

158   Shiny white glaze

Nepheline syenite	20
Dolomite	15
Whiting	3
Zinc oxide	3
Lepidolite	8
China clay	10
Flint	25
Zirconium silicate	16

In oxidation a blue white glaze with a slight speckle, clearer on porcelain. In reduction an attractive, cool, opaque, blue white.

159   Shiny white glaze

Nepheline syenite	70
Dolomite	14
Ball clay	5
Bentonite	3
Zirconium silicate	8

A white opaque glaze, breaking orange on stoneware. A whiter glaze
on stoneware, slightly blue on porcelain.

160   Broken yellow brown glaze

Whiting	20
Barium carbonate	20
Fremington clay	50
(Albany slip)	
Flint	10

In oxidation, at the lower end of the firing scale, a rich orange yellow glaze results. In reduction a more glassy, greener glaze is produced.

161   Stone speckle glaze

Feldspar	45
Whiting	15
Dolomite	5
Wood ash	5
Barium carbonate	5
Ball clay	5
China clay	10
Flint	10
Copper carbonate	0.5%

In oxidation a stone-like, speckled green glaze, greener on porcelain. In reduction a green red glaze, a muted red on porcelain.

162   Cool matt blue glaze

Feldspar (soda)	35
Whiting	19
Talc	5
Calcium borate frit	5
(Colemanite)	
China clay	18
Flint	10
Zirconium silicate	8

In reduction a cool, matt, semi-opaque blue glaze. In oxidation a whiter and more matt glaze with stone-like quality.

---

163   White mottled glaze

Feldspar	40
Whiting	5
Dolomite	40
Ball clay	10
Flint	5

A high dolomite glaze which gives a white opaque effect; cream yellow mottled in oxidation, more blue in reduction.

---

164   Smooth white glaze

Feldspar	37
Whiting	15
China clay	8
Flint	37
Bentonite	3

In oxidation a smooth white glaze. In reduction a pale blue grey stiff glaze.

Variation
With the addition of 5% vanadium pentoxide the glaze breaks a mottled grey cream in oxidation on porcelain.

---

165   White tan glaze

Nepheline syenite	60
Dolomite	25
Whiting	10
Bentonite	5

In oxidation a broken white glaze; in reduction a crackled blue-green glaze.

Variation
With an addition of 6% tin oxide a whiter glaze results, which breaks orange tan in oxidation. Do not overfire.

---

166   Semi-matt clear base glaze

Feldspar	65
Whiting	20
Flint	12
Bentonite	3

A semi-clear, matt glaze, dry on stoneware, more shiny on porcelain. In reduction a crackle pale blue.

Variation
An addition of 3% rutile (light) and 2% red iron oxide gives a ginger tan brown in reduction, a stone-like grey ginger on stoneware.

---

167   Matt white glaze

Nepheline syenite	35
Dolomite	12
Whiting	8
Zinc oxide	5
China clay	22
Flint	18

A dolomite, matt white glaze, dry and stone-like in oxidation. In reduction it is smooth and frosty; tends to pick up copper pink.

---

168   Milky white glaze

Nepheline syenite	75
Zinc oxide	3

Dolomite	5
Whiting	3
Bentonite	4
Flint	10
Antimony oxide	6%

A shiny, opaque, white glaze with a milky quality. On stoneware in oxidation at a higher range a more broken effect develops. In reduction a crackle, frosty pink green glaze results.

---

169   Semi-matt clear glaze

Feldspar	30
Whiting	30
Talc	4
China clay	18
Flint	18

In oxidation a semi-transparent, matt glaze with a slight crackle. A very pale green, clear glaze in reduction.

---

170   Stiff semi-opaque glaze

Feldspar	68
Whiting	22
Flint	6
Bentonite	4

A low alumina, semi-white, opaque glaze with a slight crackle; milky white in oxidation, milky blue in reduction.

---

171   White matt glaze

Nepheline syenite	40
Dolomite	15
Whiting	10

Ball clay	20
China clay	10
Flint	5

In oxidation a satin white, matt glaze at the low end of the temperature range and on porcelain. A dry and stone-like grey white on stoneware at higher temperatures. In reduction a smooth, matt, cream grey.

---

172   Textured cream white glaze

Feldspar	45
Whiting	33
China clay	22

In oxidation at lower temperatures a smooth, silky white and cream speckled glaze: at higher temperatures a drier, speckled glaze. In reduction a matt, slightly grey blue glaze.

---

173   Semi-opaque matt glaze

Feldspar	45
Dolomite	14
Bone ash	3
China clay	25
Flint	13

In oxidation a smooth, even, opaque white; at higher temperatures a milky white on stoneware. In reduction a stiff, milky blue, semi-matt, opaque glaze.

---

174   Cream matt speckle glaze

Cornish stone	16
Feldspar	36
Zinc oxide	5

Whiting	25
China clay	18
Zirconium silicate	10%
Ilmenite	3%

A cream white, opaque, satin matt glaze with pale brown speckles, drier on stoneware in oxidation. In reduction a pale blue, opaque, matt glaze.

---

175   White cream mottle glaze

Feldspar	38
Cornish stone	18
Whiting	18
Zinc oxide	8
China clay	18

In oxidation a white cream grey, mottled, matt glaze. In reduction a matt, slightly crazed glaze.

---

176   Matt white speckle glaze

Cornish stone	50
Whiting	6
Dolomite	23
China clay	21

In oxidation an attractive stone white, matt glaze: at the lower end of the temperature range a distinctive white speckle is formed, which becomes less clear at higher temperatures. In reduction a pale green grey matt glaze on stoneware, a matt, pale duck-egg blue on porcelain.

---

177   Matt white glaze

Nepheline syenite	35
Dolomite	14

Whiting	8
Zinc oxide	7
China clay	20
Flint	16

In oxidation a matt white glaze with iron speckles. In reduction a smooth matt glaze is formed.

Variation
With the addition of 2% copper carbonate a green glaze is formed in oxidation. In reduction a red/pink/black matt glaze is formed; bright on porcelain.

---

178   White cream glaze

Nepheline syenite	33
Whiting	8
Dolomite	18
Zinc oxide	6
China clay	20
Flint·	15

In oxidation a stone-like white matt glaze at lower temperatures on porcelain; a creamier, more speckled, stone glaze on stoneware at higher temperatures. In reduction a matt, pale green-blue glaze.

---

179   White dolomite speckle glaze

Feldspar	28
Whiting	5
Dolomite	30
Ball clay	27
Flint	10

An opaque, creamy white, dolomite glaze with small iron speckles. Smooth and even in oxidation, slightly more runny in reduction.

180   Stone, semi-matt, glaze

Feldspar	20
Whiting	30
China clay	25
Flint	25
Rutile (medium)	4%

A wide-firing glaze. In oxidation, at the lower temperatures, a semi-clear, semi-matt glaze with some gold pink flecks. At higher temperatures a more matt glaze on stoneware, smooth on porcelain. In reduction a transparent honey glaze.

181   Pale ash glaze

Wood ash	35
Feldspar	35
Ball clay	15
Talc	15

In oxidation at low temperatures a smooth, matt, pale green, speckle glaze results. At higher temperatures in oxidation and reduction a more fluxed and speckled green glaze results.

182   Semi-transparent glaze

Feldspar	35
Whiting	15
Barium carbonate	15
Ball clay	10
Flint	25

A semi-transparent, slightly crazed glaze, more matt at the lower temperature range.

Variation
Additions of iron oxide give rich pale honey and green colours.

183 White opaque glaze

Nepheline syenite	65
Dolomite	25
Ball clay	10

A matt, bright white glaze, smooth and even at lower temperatures, more broken at higher temperatures. In reduction a matt white glaze with orange flashing where the glaze is thin.

Variation
An addition of 4% tin oxide gives a more opaque white which is semi-matt.

184 Smooth opaque glaze

Cornish stone	45
Dolomite	10
Calcium borate frit (Colemanite)	5
Whiting	10
Ball clay	10
China clay	10
Flint	10

A smooth, white, satin glaze.

185 Semi-matt glaze

Petalite	60
Calcium borate frit (Colemanite)	5
Whiting	10
Talc	5
Ball clay	10

| China clay | 5 |
| Flint | 5 |

A semi-matt and stable glaze.

---

186   Semi-clear matt glaze

Feldspar *P6T — KAC*	40
Whiting	20
Ball clay	10
Flint	30

In oxidation at the lower temperature range a smooth, opaque, semi-matt white glaze with fine crazing; more clear at higher temperatures. In reduction a semi-clear, grey green glaze.

Variation
The addition of 8% red iron oxide gives a deep rich brown black glaze in reduction: a deep olive brown in oxidation.

---

187   Dolomite matt glaze

Nepheline syenite	50
Dolomite	25
Whiting	5
Ball clay	20

In oxidation a white, crystalline, matt glaze. In reduction a cream white glaze.

---

188   Matt glaze

| Whiting | 30 |
| Ball clay | 15 |

| China clay | 25 |
| Flint | 30 |

A high clay, satin, matt glaze: in oxidation a pale cream white colour, in reduction a pale blue green colour.

Variation
This glaze is good for additions of colouring oxides.

---

189   Smooth stone white cream glaze

Feldspar	50
Cornish stone	15
Whiting	16
Zinc oxide	4
Ball clay	5
China clay	10

In oxidation a smooth, white, matt glaze which breaks cream and pale blue-grey. In reduction a clear glaze.

Variation
With the addition of 4% rutile and 4% red iron oxide in oxidation a rich matt orange tan glaze results; in reduction a runny green tan.

---

190   Satin stone glaze

Feldspar	50
Whiting	20
Talc	5
Bone ash	3
Ball clay	12
China clay	10

In oxidation at lower temperature a smooth satin white and cream matt glaze; more even in colour at higher temperature. In reduction a matt pale green glaze.

Variation
With the addition of 5% rutile and 3% red iron oxide a speckle tan
cream glaze results in oxidation; in reduction a runny speckled glaze.

---

191   White dolomite glaze

Feldspar (soda)	25
Dolomite	30
Whiting	10
Ball clay	15
China clay	10
Flint	10

In oxidation a smooth, opaque, streaky white glaze. In reduction a grey
white. Do not overfire.

---

192   Semi-clear grey glaze

Cornish stone	25
Spodumene	25
Barium carbonate	5
Zinc oxide	10
Bone ash	25
Ball clay	10

In oxidation a shiny, pale, cream green grey glaze. In reduction a rich
grey with iron speckle on stoneware, smoother on porcelain.

Variation
With the addition of 6% rutile and 4% vanadium pentoxide in oxidation
a deep speckled cream tan glaze results; do not overfire. In reduction
a grey brown cream.

193   Smooth matt white glaze

Nepheline syenite	17
Feldspar	40
Whiting	4
Dolomite	18
Ball clay	11
China clay	10

A smooth white glaze in oxidation. In reduction a matt, opaque, grey cream glaze.

194   Clear pale olive green glaze

Feldspar	35
Talc	5
Whiting	20
Ball clay	20
Flint	20
Red iron oxide	1.5%

In oxidation a cool, pale, transparent, olive cream glaze. In reduction a clear transparent celadon green.

195   An ash type green yellow glaze

Calcium borate frit (Colemanite)	18
Barium carbonate	28
Lithium carbonate	5
Whiting	15
Red clay	25
Flint	9

In oxidation a mottled, streaky, bright yellow green, semi-matt glaze. In reduction a rich green speckle on stoneware; tends to bubble on porcelain.

Variation
With the addition of 1.5% red iron oxide a yellower glaze results.

---

196   Ash matt glaze

Wood ash (mixed)	40
Feldspar	40
Ball clay	20

In oxidation at lower temperatures a rich orange white, speckle glaze, smoother in colour at higher temperatures. In reduction a pale green grey matt glaze.

---

197   Semi-opaque/clear glaze

Nepheline syenite	70
Whiting	20
Flint	10

In oxidation an interesting smooth satin white when thin, more transparent when thick or on porcelain. In reduction a transparent, pale green, crackle glaze.

---

198   Smooth white opaque stone glaze

Feldspar (soda)	40
Whiting	20
Dolomite	20
Ball clay	10
China clay	10

In oxidation at lower temperatures a pale cream white stone-like glaze; smooth and more satin-like at higher temperatures. In reduction a smooth, grey white, opaque on stoneware, a pale blue green matt on porcelain.

199   Pale green cream glaze

Nepheline syenite	42
Calcium borate frit	5
(Colemanite)	
Whiting	5
Dolomite	10
Talc	12
Fremington clay	10
(Albany slip)	
Flint	16

A semi-opaque, cream green white glaze in oxidation. In reduction a mottled pale green.

Variation
With the addition of 8% rutile and 3% cobalt carbonate an opaque, silver black grey glaze results.

200   Semi-stone clear glaze

Nepheline syenite	60
Standard borax frit	10
(Ferro 3134)	
Whiting	25
Ball clay	5

On porcelain a semi-clear, on stoneware a stone cream matt glaze.

Variation
With the addition of 1.5% copper oxide a green speckle glaze results in oxidation; in reduction a green red mottle.

201   Cream opaque glaze

Feldspar	30
Whiting	5

Zinc oxide	14
Ball clay	30
Flint	21
Vanadium pentoxide	5%

A smooth, opaque, cream glaze in oxidation; tends to bubble in reduction.

* * *

Coloured and decorative glazes

※ **202   Ink blue glaze**

Volcanic ash	55
Whiting	25
Barium carbonate	10
Ball clay	10
Cobalt oxide	0.5%

In oxidation a matt, muted, satin blue grey ink colour; in reduction a bright shiny glaze, blue-black in colour.

---

203   Crystal glaze

Alkaline leadless frit	45
(Ferro 3110)	
Zinc oxide	25
Bentonite	3
Flint	19
Titanium dioxide	8

A streaky, runny, crystal glaze. In oxidation a cool grey-white on porcelain, mottled grey-orange on stoneware. In reduction a pale grey glaze. Do not overfire.

204   Orange green glaze

Fremington clay	85
(Albany clay)	
Whiting	15

In oxidation a smooth, matt and muted, orange/red/green glaze. In reduction a mottled, dark olive-brown glaze.

205   Red yellow speckle glaze

Cornish stone	48
Whiting	30
Ball clay	10
China clay	12
Red iron oxide	6%

In oxidation a smooth, satin surfaced glaze which gives a red yellow colour. In reduction a more runny, green yellow glaze results.

206   Midnight blue glaze

Feldspar	44
Whiting	17
Ball clay	8
China clay	9
Flint	22
Cobalt oxide	5%

A deep midnight blue glaze, more shiny in reduction, drier on stoneware in oxidation.

AT Δ6 STONEWARE NO CRYSTALS BUT A MATT
GLAZE RESULTS. SO-SO

207 ✸ Semi-clear crystal glaze

Nepheline syenite	40
Dolomite	15
Whiting	8
Barium carbonate	7
Flint	27
Bentonite	3
Copper oxide	1%

In oxidation a clear turquoise glaze with frothy green crystals. In reduction a muted pale green.

Variation

With 2% manganese oxide instead of the copper oxide a pale purple pink glaze with pale crystals develops, especially at the lower temperature range. In reduction a grey glaze with white crystals results on porcelain.

208   Cream grey speckle (oxidation) glaze

Feldspar (soda)	35
Spodumene	15
Whiting	25
Calcium borate frit (Colemanite)	5
China clay	20
Red iron oxide	4
Rutile	3

A smooth, opaque, matt glaze with cream yellow and grey speckles.

209   Clear green glaze

Nepheline syenite	65
Calcium borate frit (Colemanite)	30

Bentonite	5
Copper oxide	2%

In oxidation a pale, clear, medium green at low temperature range, a darker green with iron speckles at higher temperatures. In reduction a semi-clear, green red glaze.

---

210   Medium blue glaze

Feldspar	20
Calcium borate frit (Colemanite)	20
Alkaline leadless frit (Ferro 3110)	15
Ball clay	15
Flint	30
Cobalt oxide	1%
Red iron oxide	1.5%
Titanium dioxide	5%

A smooth, shiny, semi-opaque, navy blue glaze in oxidation and reduction.

---

211 ✗ Metallic black silver glaze   *No NICE 46*

Nepheline syenite	73
Zinc oxide	3
Dolomite	5
Whiting	4
China clay	4
Bentonite	3
Flint	8
Rutile (medium)	10%
Copper carbonate	4%
Ilmenite (fine)	10%

Oxidation only. A matt, metallic black glaze with silver and gold crystals.

212   Runny green brown glaze

Feldspar	36
Cornish stone	16
Whiting	24
Zinc oxide	4
China clay	20
Ilmenite	3%
Copper oxide	1.5%

In oxidation a runny, green brown glaze, which works over a wide temperature range. In reduction a runny, sticky looking glaze.

213   Wide-firing base glaze   *NO GOOD AT A6*

Nepheline syenite	73
Whiting	4
Dolomite	5
Zinc oxide	3
Bentonite	5
Flint	10

A semi-matt wide-firing base glaze. In oxidation a white opaque colour with white speckles. In reduction a semi-clear crackle glaze. A sound base glaze with which many oxides will work over a wide temperature range.

Variation 1
With the addition of 2% copper oxide a rich transparent glaze with black and gold speckles results; at higher temperatures a more matt, pinker glaze results. In reduction a rich deep dark red transparent glaze develops.

Variation 2
The addition of 3% uranium oxide in oxidation at lower temperatures gives a bright, shiny, egg yellow glaze with green patches; in reduction a shiny black glaze.

Variation 3
The addition of 1.5% cobalt oxide and 1.5% red iron oxide in oxidation

gives a mottled, blue mauve glaze, more shiny at the lower temperature range, more matt and pale at the higher range. In reduction it gives an attractive soft mottled blue mauve.

---

214   Speckle green glaze

Feldspar	38
Calcium borate frit	7
(Colemanite)	
Dolomite	7
Talc	17
Barium carbonate	8
Bentonite	5
Flint	18
Zirconium oxide	15%
Copper carbonate	2%

In oxidation at lower temperature range a pale speckle green glaze with small gold flecks; at higher temperatures a smooth, shiny, pale green iron speckle glaze on stoneware, matt on porcelain. In reduction a pale matt green.

Variation
With the addition of 10% rutile a more broken glaze is formed, which in reduction gives a speckled green and black matt glaze.

---

215   Transparent base glaze

Feldspar	40
Zinc oxide	5
Barium carbonate	8
Whiting	15
Ball clay	10
Flint	22

A clear transparent glaze.

Variation 1
With an addition of 4% red iron oxide a honey glaze results in oxidation; a green celadon in reduction.

Variation 2
With additions of 4% red iron oxide and 3% copper oxide a green brown 'oil' glaze results.

---

216   Pale green speckle glaze

Nepheline syenite	75
Zinc oxide	6
Whiting	6
Dolomite	8
Bentonite	5
Red iron oxide	0.5%
Copper oxide	0.5%

At low temperatures a bright green, semi-opaque glaze with green crystal formations. At higher temperatures a pale liquid green.

---

217   Pale purple mauve glaze

Feldspar	40
Calcium borate frit	10
(Colemanite)	
Dolomite	8
Talc	23
Bentonite	5
Flint	14
Cobalt oxide	1%

In oxidation a slightly speckled, grey/mauve/purple, matt, opaque glaze: at higher temperatures on stoneware, it tends to bubble. In reduction a smooth, slightly bluer glaze results.

DO NOT FIRE OUT AT 46

218   Matt crystal glaze

Feldspar	36
Whiting	9
Dolomite	22
Bentonite	5
Flint	28

In oxidation a smooth, matt, opaque white glaze on porcelain at the lower temperatures; a broken white speckled glaze on stoneware at higher temperatures. In reduction a cool pale matt blue glaze.

Variation

With the addition of 10% rutile (medium) a rich white glassy glaze is obtained with pink crystals in oxidation. In reduction a slightly blue glaze with white and pink crystals is obtained.

219   Pale green yellow glaze

Feldspar (soda)	38
Cornish stone	18
Zinc oxide	5
Whiting	18
Ball clay	21
Yellow ochre	5
Rutile (medium)	5

In oxidation a matt, opaque, pale green glaze with pale yellow crystals. In reduction a more shiny, brown green mottle.

220   Green crystal glaze

Feldspar	30
Whiting	9
Dolomite	17
Barium carbonate	4

China clay	12
Bentonite	3
Flint	25
Rutile (medium)	12%
Red iron oxide	6%
Ilmenite	8%
Copper oxide	1.5%

In oxidation a pale, grass green, transparent glaze with frothy, crystal, green coloured glaze forms. In reduction pale green crystals form in a pale brown background.

AT 46 BORING AT STONE WARE VERY DRY NO CRISTALS

221   Green/tan crystal glaze   *BORING   BROWN*

Nepheline syenite	75
Whiting	4
Dolomite	5
Zinc oxide	2
Bentonite	4
Flint	10
Copper oxide	2%

On porcelain in oxidation a handsome, transparent, bright green glaze, with tiny black and tan crystals, matt black when thin. In reduction a muted copper red pink is formed which gives a more attractive, burnished effect if the copper is increased by 2% to 4%.

222   Green transparent glaze

Cornish stone	45
Zinc oxide	3
Dolomite	6
China clay	17
Flint	27
Copper carbonate	2

In oxidation a soft, green coloured, semi-matt glaze. In reduction a muddy pink, matt glaze.

223   Crystal glaze

Feldspar	30
Whiting	8
Dolomite	17
Zinc oxide	12
China clay	4
Flint	22
Rutile	7

In oxidation at the lower temperature range a shiny, matt, milky white glaze with small pink crystals. If overfired the glaze becomes very runny. In reduction a lustrous blue white pearl glaze with pink and white crystals.

224   Brown-red matt glaze

Feldspar	38
Cornish stone	18
Whiting	18
Zinc oxide	6
China clay	20
Nickel oxide	5%
Red iron oxide	5%

A glaze with a wide firing range. In oxidation a matt, opaque, black/red/brown colour. Do not reduce.

225   Pale green brown speckle glaze

Feldspar	40
Cornish stone	18
Whiting	18
Zinc oxide	4
China clay	20

Rutile (dark)	5%
Copper carbonate	2%

A matt, opaque, pale green glaze running brown in oxidation. In reduction pale blue crystals form.

226   Mottled green brown matt

Feldspar	38
Cornish stone	18
Whiting	18
Zinc oxide	6
China clay	20
Copper carbonate	2%
Zirconium silicate	10%
Ilmenite	3%

A mottled, green brown, matt glaze in oxidation and reduction.

227   Streaky green glaze

Feldspar	35
Cornish stone	16
Zinc oxide	5
Whiting	25
China clay	19
Rutile (dark)	4%
Copper carbonate	1.5%
Zirconium silicate	9%
Ilmenite	2%

A smooth, pale green glaze with brown streaks in oxidation. In reduction a smooth, green brown, speckled glaze.

228   Barium base glaze

Feldspar	54
Barium carbonate	20
Dolomite	6
China clay	7
Bentonite	3
Flint	10

A frosty, smooth, white base in oxidation; a pale blue matt, which quickly picks up volatalized copper in reduction.

Variation
With an addition of 2% tin oxide and 1.5% copper oxide a pale turquoise green is obtained in oxidation, a muted opaque pink red in reduction.

229   Mottled nickel green glaze

Nepheline syenite	35
Dolomite	12
Whiting	8
Zinc oxide	5
China clay	24
Flint	16
Nickel oxide	3%

In reduction a pale green glaze with white flecks. In oxidation a dry, streaky, green brown glaze.

230   Turquoise blue matt

Nepheline syenite	40
Barium carbonate	35
Whiting	5
Lepidolite	3

China clay	10
Flint	7
Copper carbonate	2%

In oxidation a rich turquoise, matt, blue-green glaze. In reduction a muted and more mottled turquoise colour.

---

231   Semi-matt base glaze

Nepheline syenite	30
Whiting	20
Lithium carbonate	5
Ball clay	30
Flint	15

A semi-opaque, white-cream base, smooth and satin-like over porcelain, drier and more textured on stoneware.

Variation 1
With 2% red iron oxide a more yellow glaze is obtained on porcelain, a greener, greyer glaze on stoneware.

Variation 2
With an addition of 2% copper carbonate a rich green black glaze results at 1200°C, which gets darker and drier at higher temperatures. In reduction a muted pink/green glaze is obtained.

Variation 3
With the addition of 1% copper carbonate a lighter green is obtained, which breaks a paler green on porcelain. In reduction a runny bright red glaze results on porcelain, more muted on stoneware.

---

232   Turquoise glaze   *Boring △6*

Feldspar	40
Petalite	15
Barium carbonate	30
China clay	7

Flint	8
Copper carbonate	3%

In oxidation at lower temperatures a rich, matt, turquoise green glaze. In reduction a blue/red colour develops

---

233   White-cream crystal glaze

Nepheline syenite	25
Whiting	16
Zinc oxide	6
Ball clay	12
Flint	20
Rutile	15
Zirconium silicate	6

In oxidation at the lower temperature range an orange glaze with white cream crystals: at higher temperatures a more runny, muddy glaze. In reduction an orange glaze with slight frothy appearance.

---

234   Midnight blue glaze

Nepheline syenite	48
Barium carbonate	28
Whiting	14
Ball clay	10
Copper carbonate	1

A glaze with a wide firing range. Brilliant midnight blue in oxidation; in reduction a more broken blue-black on porcelain, a more blue-green on stoneware.

---

235   Muted blue glaze

Cornish stone	20
Whiting	20

Standard borax frit (Ferro 3134)	3
Fremington clay (Albany slip)	40
Ball clay	17
Copper carbonate	1%
Cobalt oxide	1%

A muted, streaky, blue-green, satin surfaced glaze. Slightly darker on stoneware in reduction.

---

236   Dark mauve glaze

Feldspar	37
Dolomite	8
Calcium borate frit (Colemanite)	7
Talc	20
Barium carbonate	7
Flint	15
Cobalt oxide	2

A cool mauve at the lower end of temperature range and in oxidation. Darker blue mauve and more attractive in reduction.

---

237   Craze-free clear base

Cornish stone	40
Whiting	15
Zinc oxide	10
China clay	15
Flint	20

In oxidation a smooth craze-free glaze; clear in oxidation, pale delicate blue in reduction.

Variation 1
An addition of 1% red iron oxide gives a pale honey in oxidation, a delicate, duck-egg blue in reduction.

Variation 2
An addition of 2% red iron oxide gives a darker honey colour in oxidation, a blue green in reduction.

Variation 3
An addition of 8% red iron oxide gives a dark ginger brown in oxidation, running a darker brown. In reduction a smooth bright black glaze develops, breaking brown on edges, on stoneware and porcelain.

---

238   Cool semi-opaque blue white base

Feldspar (soda)	50
Whiting	10
Zinc oxide	10
Barium carbonate	20
Ball clay	10

A wide-firing glaze. In oxidation a smooth, satin, matt white glaze, more stone-like on stoneware.

Variation 1
With an addition of 2% rutile, in oxidation a pale, speckled, cream white glaze: in reduction a more olive glaze.

Variation 2
With an addition of 3% rutile and 1.5% nickel oxide, in oxidation, a matt yellow glaze results. Not in reduction.

Variation 3
With the addition of 1.5% copper carbonate a rich turquoise green colour develops, with some black crystals in oxidation. In reduction a muted pink glaze results. *AG TO DRY USED BENTO. NITE IN PLACE OF BALL CLAY*

---

239   Smooth white base glaze

Feldspar	60
Whiting	5
Barium carbonate	10

Zinc oxide	5
Ball clay	10
Flint	10

A wide-firing glaze. In oxidation a semi-matt white glaze. In reduction a pale green-grey.

Variation 1
With an addition of 1.5% nickel oxide a matt rose-grey glaze develops in oxidation; a clear medium grey green in reduction.

Variation 2
An addition of 5% rutile gives a matt, flat cream pink in oxidation. In reduction a rich chun type blue-pink.

Variation 3
With addition of 1% nickel oxide and 8% titanium dioxide a matt yellow speckle develops in oxidation (not suitable for reduction).

---

240   Clear base glaze

Feldspar	40
Whiting	20
Ball clay	10
Flint	30

In oxidation a clear crackle glaze, in reduction a pale blue, stiff glaze.

Variation 1
With an addition of 1% red iron oxide a pale honey colour is achieved in oxidation, a pale green celadon in reduction.

Variation 2
An addition of 5% red iron oxide produces an olive green in oxidation, a rich dark green/brown in reduction.

Variation 3
An addition of 7% red iron oxide and 3% calcium borate frit gives a more fluxed and darker glaze, rich and shiny in reduction, more matt on stoneware in oxidation.

241   Semi-clear glaze base

Alkaline leadless frit	15
(Ferro 3110)	
Nepheline syenite	70
Whiting	10
Ball clay	5

In oxidation a semi-clear white glaze at higher temperatures, more opaque at lower temperatures. In reduction a clear crackle glaze.

Variation 1
With an addition of 2% copper oxide, a matt turquoise green glaze develops at the lower temperatures, more speckled at higher temperatures; a pink red glaze in reduction.

Variation 2
With an addition of 2% red iron oxide in oxidation a matt, pale tan glaze develops at lower temperatures, more mottled green at higher temperatures; in reduction a rich broken green.

Variation 3
With an addition of 6% red iron oxide in oxidation a matt olive ochre glaze develops, more broken at higher temperatures. In reduction a rich dark brown black.

242   Matt white base glaze

Nepheline syenite	55
Barium carbonate	20
Dolomite	5
China clay	10
Flint	10

An opaque, white, smooth, matt glaze; more satin in reduction.

Variation 1
With the addition of 2% copper carbonate a rich turquoise glaze results in oxidation, a pale matt pink in reduction.

Variation 2
Addition of 4% rutile and 4% zinc oxide gives an evenly pinholed, creamy white glaze in oxidation. In reduction an opaque white results.

Variation 3
With additions of 2% copper oxide and 1% cobalt carbonate a medium blue colour results: dry in oxidation, smother in reduction.

---

243   White matt base glaze

Feldspar	55
Whiting	15
Barium carbonate	12
China clay	10
Flint	8

A semi-opaque, white matt glaze; it gives a white − slightly blue − glaze in oxidation and a translucent matt blue in reduction. Do not overfire.

Variation 1
With 2% red iron oxide and 8% rutile a matt oatmeal glaze results in oxidation, a blue orange speckle in reduction.

Variation 2
With 5% of red iron oxide and 8% rutile a more tan coloured glaze results, shinier in reduction.

---

244   White semi-opaque base glaze

Feldspar	45
Barium carbonate	25
Dolomite	15
Whiting	5
Ball clay	5
Flint	5

In oxidation a cool white satin glaze. In reduction a grey white speckle on stoneware, a pale blue white on porcelain.

Variation 1
With the addition of 8% tin oxide and 3% bentonite a more opaque, deep white glaze results.

Variation 2
With the addition of 8% tin oxide, 3% bentonite and 3% red iron oxide a mustard yellow green glaze results. In oxidation a mottled, smooth, pale mustard glaze develops: in reduction a green mustard opaque glaze.

* * *

Green, brown and black iron glazes

245   Grey green glaze

Nepheline syenite	30
Whiting	33
Flint	32
Bentonite	5
Iron oxide	1%

In reduction a rich, grey green, speckle glaze on stoneware, a cool pale grey on porcelain. In oxidation a pale, semi-opaque, light cream colour.

246   Orange red glaze

Nepheline syenite	50
Whiting	15
Talc	5
Bone ash	10
China clay	20
Rutile (dark)	5%
Red iron oxide	4%

Colour ranges from rich orange tan to, on stoneware in reduction, mottled red tan. Do not overfire.

247   Yellow green glaze

Nepheline syenite	25
Whiting	25
Ball clay	20
China clay	10
Flint	20
Red iron oxide	2.5%

A beautiful, yellow brown, speckle glaze on porcelain at a lower temperature range. A green speckle on stoneware and opaque green on porcelain in reduction.

248   Yellow brown speckle glaze

Feldspar	35
Dolomite	11
Barium carbonate	28
Zinc oxide	17
China clay	9
Red iron oxide	3%

Rich, broken, yellow brown glaze. In oxidation a bright yellow brown glaze. In reduction a green yellow.

249   Matt black brown glaze

Nepheline syenite	44
Whiting	20
Zinc oxide	6
Ball clay	30
Nickel oxide	2%
Cobalt carbonate	2%
Red iron oxide	2%

A matt, black brown, satin surface glaze in oxidation and reduction.

250   Pale speckled wood ash glaze

Feldspar	35
Wood ash	35
China clay	25
Yellow ochre	5

In oxidation a cream brown speckle glaze which evens out at the higher temperature. In reduction a rich speckled green glaze on stoneware, a paler green on porcelain.

251   Brown black glaze

Feldspar	40
Whiting	23
Ball clay	12
Flint	25
Iron oxide	10%

A semi-transparent, brown glaze on porcelain and stoneware. In reduction, on stoneware, a rich tenmoku black glaze which breaks brown on edges.

252   Yellow green glaze

Nepheline syenite	60
Whiting	12
Fremington clay	16
(Albany slip)	
Flint	12

In reduction a crackled green, transparent glaze, lighter on porcelain. In oxidation a more yellow matt glaze, speckled white on porcelain.

253   Black brown rust glaze

Feldspar	40
Whiting	20
Zinc oxide	3
China clay	17
Flint	20
Red iron oxide	10%

A slightly runny glaze, a rich black brown tenmoku in reduction, a lighter rust red glaze in oxidation. Do not overfire.

254   Rust red brown glaze

Feldspar	50
Whiting	20
Zinc oxide	4
China clay	11
Flint	15
Iron oxide	10%

A broken red brown rust glaze in oxidation; a rich broken tenmoku on stoneware in reduction.

255   Broken brown glaze

Feldspar	40
Whiting	19
Zinc oxide	3
China clay	18
Flint	20
Red iron oxide	10%

An even red brown glaze in oxidation and reduction.

256   Satin black glaze

Nepheline syenite	15
Barium carbonate	10
Talc	15
Fremington clay	60
Chromium oxide	1%
Cobalt oxide	2%
Manganese oxide	2%

A satin, matt black glaze with a green tinge to edges. Stable and even over a wide temperature range in oxidation and reduction.

257   Dark brown black matt glaze

Feldspar	50
Whiting	5
Dolomite	22
China clay	23
Red iron oxide	9%

A dark brown, muted glaze, matt and opaque. Darker on stoneware in reduction.

258   Red brown glaze

Feldspar	26
Ball clay	20
Whiting	20
Flint	34
Red iron oxide	10%

In oxidation at 1200°C (2192°F) a deep semi-transparent brown glaze running to black; at higher temperatures the colour deepens slightly; it is more translucent on porcelain and redder in colour. In reduction a good, hard, black glaze breaking to brown on edges.

259   Matt terracotta glaze

Nepheline syenite	50
Cornish stone	12
Whiting	15
Zinc oxide	3
Ball clay	20
Red iron oxide	6%
Rutile	4%

Do not apply too thickly. A rich, decorative, matt, terracotta red with yellow streaks on stoneware. Runny on porcelain, but the colour is interesting.

260   Speckled yellow brown glaze

Nepheline syenite	50
Whiting	4
Dolomite	18
China clay	24
Zirconium oxide	2
Red iron oxide	2

In oxidation a matt, opaque, speckled yellow brown glaze on stoneware and porcelain. In reduction an opaque, green yellow glaze, darker on stoneware, which if overfired has a tendency to run.

261   Dark brown glaze

Cornish stone	30
Whiting	10
Fremington clay	60
(Albany slip)	
Iron oxide	8%

A high clay slip glaze. In oxidation at low temperatures a dark green brown glaze which becomes darker at higher temperatures. In reduction a runny, bright brown glaze, going green when thick.

---

262   Brown matt glaze

Whiting	10
Zinc oxide	20
Fremington clay	70
(Albany slip)	

A high clay slip glaze; in oxidation it gives a smooth, opaque, mustard yellow. In reduction it gives a dark brown, slightly streaky glaze.

✱263   **Pale green celadon glaze**   *Δ6 Boring*

Nepheline syenite	70
Whiting	14
Flint	14
Bentonite	2
Red iron oxide	2

In oxidation a pale crackle yellow glaze, transparent on porcelain, drier on stoneware. In reduction a rich pale green grey crackle on porcelain, a dark celadon green brown on stoneware.

---

264   Matt yellow glaze

Feldspar	35
Dolomite	11
Barium carbonate	25
Ball clay	8
Flint	6
Zirconium silicate	15
Red iron oxide	6%

In oxidation a matt, opaque, yellow orange glaze, very bright on porcelain. In reduction a smoother, more muted, yellow olive glaze.

265   Brown ginger glaze

Feldspar	52
Whiting	12
Barium carbonate	4
Zinc oxide	3
Flint	25
Bentonite	4
Red iron oxide	5%

A clear, transparent, dark honey glaze over porcelain, in reduction a dark, transparent, holly green on porcelain, a shiny green brown on stoneware. In oxidation a broken, mottled brown glaze on stoneware.

266   Dark green brown glaze

Nepheline syenite	13
Feldspar	24
Dolomite	5
Whiting	11
China clay	15
Flint	22
Bentonite	2
Red iron oxide	8

In oxidation a semi-shiny, dark green glaze which breaks brown, over a wide temperature range; more red on porcelain. In reduction a more shiny black glaze which breaks rich brown on edges.

267   Streaky rust glaze

Feldspar	38
Cornish stone	18

Whiting	18
Zinc oxide	7
China clay	19
Red iron oxide	8%

In oxidation a matt, rusty brown glaze over a wide temperature range.
In reduction a brown green, streaky glaze.

---

268   Brown speckle ash glaze

Wood ash (mixed)	40
Feldspar	40
Ball clay	20
Ilmenite	4%

In oxidation a brown, semi-transparent, runny, speckle glaze at lower
temperatures. In the higher range a more matt glaze, grey on stoneware,
cream brown speckle on porcelain. In reduction a clear, runny, transparent brown glaze.

---

269   Brown speckle stone glaze

Nepheline syenite	27
Dolomite	15
Whiting	7
Zinc oxide	6
China clay	25
Flint	20
Ilmenite	10%

In oxidation a matt, bright, opaque glaze, white with a light brown
speckle. In reduction a matt, smooth, opaque, speckled glaze.

---

270   Transparent red brown glaze

| Feldspar (soda) | 15 |
| Feldspar | 16 |

Whiting	15
Barium carbonate	5
Zinc oxide	5
Ball clay	12
Flint	32
Red iron oxide	8%

In oxidation at the lower temperatures a rich, transparent, treacle brown glaze. At higher temperatures a more broken red brown colour. In reduction the brown is slightly deeper.

Variation
If 1.5% nickel oxide is added to replace the iron oxide a pale pink brown transparent glaze results.

---

271   Clear blue green glaze

Feldspar	20
Wood ash	5
Whiting	20
Talc	5
China clay	20
Flint	30
Red iron oxide	2%

In oxidation a pale, clear, honey coloured glaze; without the iron oxide a clear transparent glaze. In reduction a pale blue green glaze; without the iron oxide a watery blue green.

---

272   Matt iron glaze

Feldspar (soda)	45
Whiting	15
Ball clay	12
China clay	8
Flint	10
Red iron oxide	10

In oxidation a smooth, matt, green yellow black glaze. In reduction a smooth red brown glaze, deeper red on stoneware.

---

273   Deep brown black glaze

Feldspar	30
Feldspar (soda)	30
Whiting	10
Dolomite	5
Ball clay	8
Flint	17
Red iron oxide	6%
Cobalt oxide	1%
Manganese oxide	3%

In oxidation a deep clear brown black on stoneware; a deep green black on porcelain. In reduction a rich brown green.

---

274   Iron glaze

Cornish stone	45
Whiting	12
Dolomite	5
Ball clay	12
Flint	26
Red iron oxide	6%

A smooth, shiny glaze. In oxidation an olive green glaze at the lower temperatures, a rich deep olive brown at higher temperatures. In reduction a rich holly green.

Variation
With the further addition of 3% red iron oxide a deep black brown colour results.

275   Semi-matt iron glaze

Fremington clay	80
(Albany slip)	
Spodumene	10
Yellow ochre	10

A high clay slip glaze; in oxidation at lower temperatures a dark red brown glaze with 'oil spots' if applied thickly. At higher temperatures a bright tan brown colour develops. In reduction a smooth even brown.

276   Transparent green glaze

Feldspar	75
Whiting	15
China clay	5
Flint	5
Iron oxide	4%

In oxidation a thick, clear, honey coloured glaze with a crackle; in reduction a rich shiny green.

277   Pale green celadon glaze

Feldspar	25
Wood ash	20
Whiting	18
Red clay	12
Flint	25

In oxidation at the lower temperature range, a smooth, pale, speckled cream green, more clear at higher temperatures. In reduction a rich celadon semi-opaque glaze.

278   Cool green glaze

Nepheline syenite	55
Whiting	10
Fremington clay	25
(Albany slip)	
Flint	10
Red iron oxide	2%
Zirconium silicate	5%

In oxidation a smooth, matt, pale green glaze, speckled brown when thin. In reduction a rich, semi-matt, medium green brown glaze.

279   Rich olive glaze

Feldspar	55
Whiting	10
Fremington clay	35
(Albany slip)	
Red iron oxide	3%

In oxidation at the lower temperature range, a mottled olive, matt/shiny glaze; at higher temperatures a rich red green glaze on stoneware, a deep olive on porcelain. In reduction a rich green brown, shiny glaze.

280   Speckled matt black glaze

Fremington clay	97
(Albany slip)	
Cobalt oxide	3

A smooth, speckled, matt black glaze, more speckled in reduction.

281   Mottled tan brown matt glaze

Fremington clay	80
(Albany slip)	
Dolomite	10
Whiting	10

A high clay glaze. In oxidation a mottled tan brown glaze, more red coloured at higher temperatures. In reduction a dark olive tan glaze.

282   Mirror brown glaze

Nepheline syenite	15
Fremington clay	85
(Albany slip)	

A bright, shiny, brown glaze in oxidation and reduction.

283   Black brown matt glaze

Lepidolite	5
Fremington clay	85
(Albany slip)	
Yellow ochre	10

A matt glaze with light gold brown and black speckles. Stable at higher temperatures in oxidation and reduction, but lighter in colour.

High Firing Stoneware Glazes 1250 °C ~ 1280 °C (2282 °F ~ 2336 °F) Orton cones 7, 8 and 9

Transparent and semi-transparent glazes

---

284   Semi-opaque white glaze

Feldspar (soda)	60
Dolomite	10
China clay	20
Flint	10

Bright, even, white glaze over porcelain. In oxidation, a cream opaque colour over stoneware. In reduction a semi-clear glaze.

---

285   Semi-opaque bright white glaze

Feldspar	60
Dolomite	20
China clay	10
Flint	10

A frosty, semi-opaque, bright glaze with a slightly crazed surface. Thicker application gives a more opaque glaze. In reduction a clear glaze.

286   Smooth matt glaze

Feldspar (soda)	35
Whiting	10
Dolomite	20
China clay	5
Flint	30

In oxidation a smooth, opaque, matt glaze. In reduction a clear glaze with a smooth, white, crystal, opaque surface where thicker.

287   Semi-clear glaze

Feldspar	40
Cornish stone	20
Whiting	20
Zinc oxide	3
China clay	8
Ball clay	9

In oxidation a semi-opaque, blue-white, bubbly glaze. In reduction a clear transparent glaze.

288   Semi-transparent glaze

Feldspar	40
Whiting	8
Dolomite	12
Ball clay	10
Flint	30

In oxidation a semi-shiny glaze with milk white flecks. In reduction a semi-clear, shiny glaze.

289   Semi-matt clear glaze

Feldspar	40
Whiting	20
China clay	25
Flint	15

In oxidation a semi-matt glaze; in reduction a slightly more clear glaze.

290   Clear milky glaze

Feldspar	65
Whiting	20
Flint	15
Bentonite	3%

In oxidation a clear glaze which is slightly milky where thick. In reduction a more transparent glaze.

291   Clear runny glaze

Feldspar	65
Cornish stone	10
Whiting	20
Zinc oxide	5

In oxidation a clear glaze on porcelain, a semi-clear matt on stoneware. In reduction a clear crackle glaze.

292   Semi-clear transparent glaze

Feldspar	25
Whiting	15

Ball clay	34
Flint	20
Yellow ochre	6

A high clay glaze which is smooth and semi-transparent. In oxidation a pale cream colour is obtained, brighter on porcelain. In reduction a pale blue green.

---

293   Semi-clear matt glaze

Nepheline syenite	40
Whiting	20
Ball clay	10
Flint	30

A useful variation on the basic clear Leach cone 8 glaze; slightly more matt on edges. A tendency to craze.

---

294   Frothy white clear glaze

Feldspar	40
Whiting	15
Talc	15
Flint	25
Bentonite	5

A low alumina, high silica glaze: in reduction a stiff, clear, transparent glaze, opaque white where thick. In oxidation a dry glaze.

---

295   Stiff transparent glaze

Feldspar	20
Nepheline syenite	22
Whiting	8
Dolomite	5

Barium carbonate	10
Ball clay	10
Flint	20
Zirconium silicate	5

Slightly bubbled, clear glaze in oxidation; a stiff, crackle, transparent glaze, pale green, in reduction.

296   Semi-translucent blue glaze

Nepheline syenite	40
Whiting	8
Dolomite	10
Talc	8
Flint	30
Bentonite	4

In reduction a deep blue-white glaze, breaking to clear on edges. In oxidation a slightly cream coloured glaze with a drier surface.

297   Clear ash glaze

Cornish stone	35
Wood ash	55
Fremington clay	10
(Albany slip)	

In oxidation a pale honey clear glaze, which crazes slightly. In reduction a pale green mottled glaze.

298   Pale green clear glaze

Nepheline syenite	40
Whiting	16
Dolomite	5

Ball clay	14
Flint	25

A crazed, slightly green coloured glaze on porcelain, more even on stoneware. Dry and semi-matt in oxidation.

---

299   Clear transparent glaze

Nepheline syenite	30
Whiting	15
Talc	5
Zinc oxide	5
Ball clay	10
Flint	35

A well fitting glaze, craze-free.

Variation
With the addition of 5% red iron oxide rich yellow and red colours result.

---

300   Pale blue with iron speckle glaze

Nepheline syenite	15
Whiting	3
Dolomite	22
China clay	38
Flint	22

Reduction only. A smooth, high clay matt glaze; pale blue on porcelain, pale blue with iron speckle on stoneware.

---

301   Blue-green crackle glaze

Nepheline syenite	42
Whiting	19

China clay	14
Flint	25
Yellow ochre	2.5%

A clear crackle glaze. In oxidation a pale honey, crackle glaze, tending to be dry on stoneware. In reduction a rich clear crackle blue-green glaze, similar on porcelain to the Chinese Ying Ching glaze.

---

302   Semi-clear glaze

Feldspar	70
Whiting	10
Dolomite	5
Talc	5
Bentonite	4
Flint	6

In oxidation a semi-clear, slightly crackled and cream-coloured glaze. In reduction a pale, light green, transparent glaze.

---

303   Clear glaze

Feldspar	65
Whiting	5
Talc	6
Bone ash	4
China clay	3
Flint	12
Bentonite	5

A clear glaze with a slight crackle; in reduction a pale blue-green.

---

304   Semi-clear chun glaze

Feldspar	77
Talc	6

Dolomite	6
Flint	6
Bone ash	5

In oxidation a stiff, semi-opaque, grey chun glaze. In reduction a semi-opaque, pale blue-green glaze with slight crackle.

305   Stiff crackle glaze

Feldspar	80
Whiting	10
Flint	10

A stiff, semi-clear, crackle glaze. White with a strong crackle on porcelain, drier on stoneware in oxidation; very light blue with small crackle in reduction.

306   Satin clear glaze

Feldspar	75
Nepheline syenite	8
Wood ash	12
China clay	5

A smooth satin, semi-matt glaze with a slight crackle; slightly cream coloured and drier in oxidation; smooth and slightly blue in reduction.

307   Stiff opaque glaze

Feldspar	60
Whiting	10
Flint	30

A stiff, high silica glaze. Milky white semi-matt in oxidation, milky blue in reduction.

◀ Porcelain bowl with
nickel glaze 404,
oxidized ▼

Stoneware pot with nickel glaze 404, oxidized

Porcelain lidded pot with glaze 410 (clotted blood red variation), oxidized

Porcelain bowl with glaze 411 (Frankenstein red variation), oxidized

308   Clear crackle glaze

Feldspar	40
Whiting	20
China clay	15
Flint	25

In reduction a strong-surfaced, slightly blue-tinted glaze with a crackle. A duller, semi-transparent, matt glaze in oxidation.

309   Delicate chun glaze

Feldspar	46
Dolomite	6
Zinc oxide	6
Whiting	10
China clay	2
Flint	30

A clear transparent glaze which forms optical blue where thick. Good over black clay slip.

310   Clear glaze

Nepheline syenite	36
Whiting	3
Dolomite	17
Zinc oxide	2
Ball clay	6
Flint	36

A clear glaze with a slight crackle.

311   Smooth semi-clear glaze

Lepidolite	60
Wollastonite	5
Zinc oxide	2
Talc	5
Ball clay	8
Flint	20

A good semi-clear glaze.

312   Semi-clear glaze

Feldspar	45
Whiting	15
Ball clay	12
China clay	8
Flint	20

A stiff semi-clear glaze. In reduction a smooth, crazed, semi-clear glaze. In oxidation a stiff, semi-opaque, cream white glaze.

313   Smooth semi-clear glaze

Feldspar (soda)	63
Whiting	20
China clay	7
Flint	10

A smooth semi-clear glaze with slight crazing. In oxidation, cool, cream-white glaze. In reduction a pale blue, clear glaze.

314   Bright clear glaze

Feldspar	30
Whiting	15
Dolomite	7
Ball clay	10
China clay	8
Flint	30

A smooth, bright, clear glaze, cream-white on stoneware and porcelain in oxidation. In reduction a clear pale blue transparent glaze.

315   Clear glaze

Feldspar	50
Whiting	14
Barium carbonate	3
Zinc oxide	3
Ball clay	10
Flint	20

A smooth, transparent glaze. In oxidation a clear, colourless, transparent glaze. In reduction a pale blue grey colour.

Variation
With an addition of 0.5% chromium oxide a cool, transparent, green glaze results.

316   Cool celadon glaze

Feldspar	30
Whiting	20
Ball clay	20
Flint	30
Red iron oxide	1%

A pale, clear, transparent, honey coloured glaze in oxidation. In reduction a pale green celadon.

317   Semi-clear glaze

Feldspar	40
Whiting	25
China clay	10
Flint	25

In oxidation a semi-clear glaze, more opaque when thick. In reduction a pale blue-grey, semi-clear glaze, transparent when thin.

318   Pale cream/blue glaze

Feldspar	65
Wood ash	10
Whiting	10
Ball clay	6
Flint	9
Red iron oxide	1%

A clear glaze, pale cream in oxidation. In reduction a pale blue-grey colour with iron speckles.

319   Blue-grey chun glaze

Feldspar	40
Whiting	9
Barium carbonate	8
Zinc oxide	4
Bone ash	4
Ball clay	5
Flint	30
Red iron oxide	1.5%

A semi-clear glaze with a chun effect. In reduction a muted, creamy coloured base with pale blue flecks. In reduction a subtle, blue-grey glaze.

* * *

Opaque, matt, white, cream glazes

---

320   Stone matt glaze

Feldspar (soda)	54
Whiting	3
Dolomite	18
China clay	25

A semi-opaque, stone matt glaze in oxidation; slightly more speckled in reduction.

---

321   Stone matt glaze

Feldspar	30
Dolomite	30
Whiting	5
China clay	30
Flint	5

A dolomite matt glaze; hard and stone-like in reduction; slightly drier in oxidation.

Variation
Substitution of ball clay for china clay will give a good, opaque, dolomite, white glaze in oxidation.

---

322   White glaze

Feldspar	40
Whiting	20
Ball clay	5
China clay	5

Flint	20
Titanium dioxide	10

In oxidation an even, white glaze. In reduction a mottled, opaque, blue-white glaze.

---

323   Cool matt glaze

Feldspar	55
Dolomite	5
Barium carbonate	20
China clay	10
Flint	10

A cool, barium matt glaze, pale blue-white in oxidation, slightly clear in reduction.

Variation
This glaze is a good base for added colouring oxides.

---

324   Stiff white opaque glaze

Feldspar	65
Whiting	10
China clay	25

In oxidation an opaque, stiff, white glaze with air bubbles and crackle; more even over porcelain. In reduction a semi-opaque glaze.

---

325   Smooth ash glaze

Feldspar	40
Wood ash	40
Ball clay	20

A smooth ash glaze; in oxidation on porcelain a smooth, cream-white, slightly brown speckle glaze. In reduction a slightly green effect.

326   Tin white glaze

Feldspar	50
Whiting	25
China clay	15
Flint	10
Tin oxide	8%

A smooth, white, opaque glaze; milky in oxidation. In reduction an opaque, pale green-grey glaze.

327   Stone semi-matt glaze

Nepheline syenite	50
Whiting	25
China clay	10
Flint	15
Tin oxide	8%
Yellow ochre	2.5%

A stone, opaque, white, matt glaze. In oxidation a dry stone-like surface develops with pink/orange speckles, smooth on porcelain. In reduction a bright green-grey opaque glaze.

328   Matt yellow blue glaze

Cornish stone	20
Whiting	20
Fremington clay	40
(Albany slip)	
China clay	20
Copper oxide	1%
Cobalt oxide	1%

A high clay, wide firing, smooth, matt, opaque glaze which can be applied raw. In oxidation a blue/green mottled glaze. In reduction a darker blue, breaking green.

329   Bright yellow-cream glaze

Nepheline syenite	45
Whiting	18
Talc	5
Bone ash	10
Calcium borate frit (Colemanite)	2
Ball clay	20
Red iron oxide	3%

A smooth, matt, yellow-cream coloured glaze. In oxidation a muted green-yellow, on porcelain a rich warm yellow orange. In reduction a brown-yellow. Do not overfire.

330   High clay semi-matt glaze

Feldspar	30
Lopidolite	12
Dolomite	20
Ball clay	8
China clay	20
Flint	10

In reduction a smooth, even, semi-matt clear glaze, slightly green. In oxidation on stoneware, a stiff, more opaque glaze; on porcelain a smooth, slightly cream-coloured matt glaze.

331   White opaque matt glaze

Feldspar (soda)	28
Nepheline syenite	32
Dolomite	9
Barium carbonate	11

| China clay | 12 |
| Flint | 8 |

A smooth, white, opaque, matt glaze. In oxidation an even, white, matt glaze on porcelain; on stoneware a drier matt. In reduction a semi-transparent, matt, opaque glaze.

---

332 Blue grey opaque glaze

Nepheline syenite	50
Whiting	4
Talc	30
Ball clay	8
Flint	8

In reduction a smooth, opaque, subdued blue grey glaze. In oxidation a pale beige tan glaze.

---

333 Smooth speckled white tan glaze

Nepheline syenite	20
Cornish stone	17
Whiting	5
Dolomite	15
Talc	16
China clay	24
Flint	3

A smooth, high clay glaze. In oxidation a matt grey-white with orange tan speckles on stoneware, a smooth speckled tan glaze on porcelain. In reduction a white, more opaque glaze.

Variation
The substitution of ball clay for china clay will give a more mottled and slightly lower firing glaze.

334   Matt white glaze

Feldspar (soda)	55
Whiting	17
Zinc oxide	4
China clay	16
Flint	8

A smooth, matt, semi-opaque, white glaze.

335   Milky white opaque glaze

Feldspar (soda)	40
Whiting	20
Standard borax frit (Ferro 3134)	10
Flint	30

A smooth, stiff, milky, white, low clay, opaque glaze which goes clear on edges. Slightly more clear in reduction.

336   Satin white matt glaze

Feldspar (soda)	65
Dolomite	6
Zinc oxide	18
China clay	6
Flint	5

An opaque white glaze. In oxidation a more opaque white on stoneware, more smooth on porcelain. In reduction a semi-opaque with white crystal formations when thick.

---

337   Semi-opaque glaze

Feldspar	25
Cornish stone	20
Whiting	10
Dolomite	10
Talc	8
China clay	20
Flint	7

A smooth, semi-matt glaze. In oxidation a creamy matt opaque glaze on stoneware, on porcelain a more vellum glaze. In reduction a semi-opaque glaze.

---

338   White speckle matt glaze

Feldspar (soda)	35
Whiting	28
China clay	28
Flint	9

A smooth, semi-opaque glaze with a white speckle. In oxidation the speckle is brighter and more noticeable: on porcelain a rich deep quality develops. In reduction the glaze becomes more frosty and the speckles less pronounced.

---

339   Stone white glaze

Nepheline syenite	55
Dolomite	20
Whiting	3
China clay	22

A stone white matt glaze with slight orange speckles. Works well on stoneware and porcelain.

340   Speckled cream glaze

Nepheline syenite	45
Whiting	5
Dolomite	8
Barium carbonate	20
Ball clay	10
Flint	12
Titanium dioxide	8%

Reduction only. On stoneware, a speckled cream white where thick, an orange yellow speckle where thin. A pink white glaze over a porcelain body.

341   Dolomite white glaze

Nepheline syenite	17
Dolomite	23
Whiting	5
China clay	35
Flint	20

A smooth, opaque, satin matt glaze in reduction. Opaque when thick, iron speckle when thin. Cream white opaque in oxidation.

342   Matt speckle glaze

Nepheline syenite	40
Dolomite	20
Whiting	10
Ball clay	30

A stone matt speckle effect on stoneware, a smooth white speckle on porcelain, in oxidation. A rich dolomite matt glaze with speckle in reduction; on porcelain it gives a matt, pale green, opaque glaze.

---

343   Speckled ash glaze

Nepheline syenite	30
Wood ash	30
Dolomite	10
Red clay	10
China clay	10
Flint	10

In oxidation, a dry cream/grey glaze on stoneware; a speckled cream white on porcelain. In reduction, a speckled dark green glaze on stoneware, a runny rich crazed green glaze on porcelain.

---

344   Speckled white-green glaze

Feldspar	50
Dolomite	20
Whiting	5
China clay	20
Fremington clay	5
(Albany slip)	

In oxidation a smooth, white green speckle glaze, very cool and attractive on porcelain. In reduction a pale green colour on porcelain, a matt speckled glaze on stoneware.

---

345   Opaque speckle glaze

Feldspar	30
Feldspar (soda)	10
Calcium borate frit	10
(Colemanite)	
Dolomite	8
Talc	14

| Ball clay | 8 |
| Flint | 20 |

In reduction a hard-surfaced, white opaque glaze; iron speckles on stoneware, pale blue on porcelain. Slightly too stiff in oxidation.

---

346   Runny green glaze

Nepheline syenite	40
Calcium borate frit (Colemanite)	10
Dolomite	8
Talc	13
Ball clay	9
Flint	20

In reduction, a shiny green glaze, with speckles on stoneware. In reduction, a semi-clear glaze on stoneware, a pale matt cream on porcelain.

---

347   Matt white orange peel glaze

Feldspar	35
Dolomite	15
Barium carbonate	25
Ball clay	10
Zirconium silicate	15
Tin oxide	6%

An opaque, matt white glaze, stony in oxidation; slightly more blue in reduction.

---

348   Dry stone glaze

Wood ash	25
Cement	25
China clay	50

A textured, dry, orange yellow, matt glaze which must be used immediately it is mixed, or else it sets. The high clay content tends to make it crawl.

---

349   Mottled blue-cream glaze

Feldspar	35
Whiting	10
Dolomite	20
Bentonite	5
Flint	30
Rutile	8%

In reduction a shiny glaze with blue streaks and white crystals. Do not overfire. In oxidation a pink salmon, running to speckle green.

---

350   Silky jade glaze

Feldspar	35
Barium carbonate	10
Calcium borate frit	7
(Colemanite)	
Dolomite	8
Talc	20
Bentonite	4
Flint	16

A silky jade matt glaze, yellow and creamy in oxidation, pale green in reduction.

---

351   Semi-matt glaze

Whiting	34
China clay	33
Flint	33

A low alumina glaze which runs transparent. In oxidation a more matt, cream coloured glaze. In reduction a watery, clear blue with a slight crackle.

---

352   Silky matt glaze

Feldspar	33
Whiting	20
Ball clay	13
China clay	20
Flint	14

A high clay slip glaze. In oxidation a silky, semi-opaque, creamy matt glaze, drier on stoneware. In reduction a pale sea green, blue, silky glaze with a slight crackle.

---

353   Smooth white glaze

Feldspar (soda)	35
Whiting	18
Ball clay	8
China clay	25
Flint	14

A high clay glaze, semi-opaque white, slightly green white in reduction. In oxidation a dry, opaque glaze.

---

354   Opaque smooth semi-matt white

Feldspar	35
Whiting	18
Ball clay	8
China clay	24
Flint	15

Porcelain bowl with glaze 221, oxidized

Porcelain bowl with glaze 380 (variation 2), oxidized

Porcelain bowl with glaze 213 (variation 2), with a band of black pigment which ran into the glaze during firing

Porcelain bowl with glaze 218 plus 10% rutile to give rich pink crystals

In reduction a rich, smooth surfaced, opaque, silky white glaze, with a slight green tint. In oxidation, a dry, opaque, milky white glaze.

---

355   Matt cream white glaze

Nepheline syenite	50
Whiting	20
Zinc oxide	3
Ball clay	10
Flint	17

In oxidation a stone white cream glaze on porcelain, a drier grey white on stoneware. In reduction a crackle transparent glaze.

---

356   Stone glaze

Feldspar (soda)	55
Whiting	23
Ball clay	10
China clay	12

A high clay glaze which gives a smooth, opaque matt effect. In oxidation, a cream colour glaze on porcelain, a crawled cream-white on stoneware. In reduction a pale blue matt glaze.

Variation
An addition of 1.5% chromium oxide gives a matt green colour, dull in oxidation, brighter in reduction.

---

357   Smooth pale cream-green glaze

Feldspar	36
Calcium borate frit	7
(Colemanite)	
Dolomite	7

Talc	18
Barium carbonate	9
Bentonite	5
Flint	18

A smooth matt glaze. In oxidation it gives a pale cream on porcelain, but bubbles slightly on stoneware. In reduction a pale opaque blue-green Chinese celadon is obtained.

358   Semi-opaque white glaze

Nepheline syenite	35
Dolomite	15
Whiting	5
Ball clay	10
Flint	35

A smooth, hard, semi-opaque, white glaze.

359   Matt white glaze

Wollastonite	50
Ball clay	15
China clay	35

A high clay slip glaze which is a smooth, even, opaque white. A thick application will encourage small white crystals to form.

360   Matt cream-brown glaze

Nepheline syenite	25
Talc	35
Whiting	15
Ball clay	25

A smooth, matt, cream-brown glaze.

361   Smooth cream speckle glaze

Feldspar	40
Talc	15
Whiting	15
China clay	15
Ball clay	15

A smooth, opaque, matt glaze; in oxidation a pale creamy white speckle glaze develops, lighter on porcelain. In reduction, on stoneware, it becomes yellow ochre in colour with iron speckles, and softer in colour on porcelain.

362   Milky white opaque glaze

Feldspar	67
Calcium borate frit (Colemanite)	4
Barium carbonate	10
Zinc oxide	4
Whiting	10
Bentonite	5

A smooth, opaque, matt white glaze; in oxidation a dry matt. In reduction a more shiny blue white glaze.

363   Stone matt glaze

Nepheline syenite	65
Whiting	18
Ball clay	9
Flint	8

In oxidation a stone-like matt on porcelain, a speckled stone on stoneware. In reduction a semi-clear crazed glaze; pale grey on stoneware, a clear grey-green on porcelain.

364   White-orange matt glaze

Feldspar	32
Dolomite	18
Spodumene	22
Ball clay	16
China clay	12

A smooth matt glaze, creamy white in oxidation, speckled and pale blue grey in reduction on stoneware.

Variation
With the addition of 4% tin oxide in oxidation, a matt, opaque, orange-white speckle glaze results. In reduction an opaque white with iron speckles on stoneware, a smooth white-orange on porcelain.

365   Stiff mottled glaze

Feldspar	40
Whiting	16
Talc	11
Ball clay	8
Flint	25

A semi-opaque, smooth glaze. In oxidation a transparent glaze with white crystals on stoneware, more opaque on porcelain. In reduction a fatty blue-grey opaque glaze.

366   Smooth white glaze

Feldspar	45
Dolomite	20
Whiting	10
Ball clay	25

In oxidation a dry stone white matt glaze on stoneware, smooth and speckled on porcelain. In reduction a satin-surfaced cream glaze with iron speckles on stoneware, more even on porcelain.

367   Smooth white glaze

Feldspar	50
Dolomite	20
Whiting	5
Ball clay	20
Flint	5

In oxidation a smooth, dry, stone white glaze on stoneware, speckled cream on porcelain. In reduction a satin speckle glaze with iron spots on stoneware, smooth on porcelain.

368   Creamy white glaze

Feldspar	68
Whiting	20
Red clay	7
China clay	5
Titanium dioxide	8%

A smooth, creamy white glaze. In oxidation a creamy white colour with small pale pink crystals. In reduction a more satin-like glaze.

369   Pale grey tan glaze

Nepheline syenite	60
Fremington clay	26
Flint	10
Zirconium silicate	4

A smooth glaze, in oxidation a tan orange colour. In reduction a deep grey-white, tan orange where thin.

370   Semi-clear white glaze

Nepheline syenite	25
Whiting	15
Zinc oxide	15
China clay	15
Flint	30

A wide-firing glaze. In oxidation an attractive, semi-clear, milky white glaze, speckled on stoneware. In reduction a clear, pale blue-grey glaze.

Variation
With the addition of 5% rutile a grey pink glaze results which runs opalescent blue in oxidation. In reduction a dark mottled blue-grey black.

371   Semi-matt soapy glaze

Feldspar	40
Calcium borate frit	8
(Colemanite)	
Dolomite	8
Talc	19
Bentonite	5
Flint	20

A cool, opaque glaze. In oxidation a stiff cream-white glaze. In reduction a smooth, grey-white, soapy glaze.

372   Semi-opaque mottle glaze

Feldspar	20
Whiting	23
Talc	10
China clay	10

Flint	37
Zirconium silicate	10%

A shiny, semi-opaque, mottle white glaze in oxidation. In reduction a pale green grey glaze.

---

373   Shiny white glaze

Feldspar	76
Zinc oxide	12
Ball clay	12

In oxidation a white, opaque, semi-matt, dry glaze. In reduction a shiny opaque white.

* * *

Coloured glazes

---

374   Grey green glaze

Feldspar	65
Dolomite	22
Flint	3
Ball clay	10
Cobalt oxide	0.5%
Chrome oxide	1.5%

A semi-opaque, satin, grey-green glaze. Speckled on stoneware in reduction. A greyer colour in oxidation.

---

375   Bright grass green glaze

Feldspar	50
Dolomite	5

Barium carbonate	25
China clay	10
Flint	10
Iron oxide	4%
Copper oxide	1%

In oxidation an opaque, speckled, grass green glaze, very bright on porcelain or a light coloured body. In reduction a dark, opaque, red-brown glaze.

376   Copper glaze   *RED) ⚹ NOT NICE RED*

Nepheline syenite	53
Whiting	14
Zinc oxide	6
Talc	5
China clay	6
Flint	16
Copper carbonate	3%
Tin oxide	3%

A mottle black green brown glaze in oxidation; a pink green glaze in reduction.

377   Jade green glaze

Feldspar	36
Calcium borate frit	8
(Colemanite)	
Barium carbonate	10
Dolomite	7
Talc	20
Flint	15
Bentonite	4

A silky glaze which fires a pale green matt in reduction, a pale cream in oxidation.

Variation
An addition of 20% zirconium silicate gives a white speckle, silky matt glaze in oxidation.

---

378   Copper red-green glaze   *VERY NICE A6 OX*

~~RED~~

		NOT NICE RED
Nepheline syenite	35	
Whiting	20	
Zinc oxide	5	
Barium carbonate	10	
Flint	30	
Tin oxide	5%	
Copper carbonate	2%	

In reduction a deep blood red glaze with green specks on porcelain. Do not overfire. In oxidation a rich green turquoise; it will mature at 1200°C (2192°F).

---

379   Grey blue glaze

Feldspar (soda)	26
Whiting	15
Talc	10
China clay	14
Flint	20
Zirconium silicate	15
Cobalt oxide	1.5%
Nickel oxide	2%

A satin, opaque, grey blue glaze, lighter in oxidation, more speckled and deeper colour in reduction.

---

380   Speckled base glaze

Feldspar	32
Whiting	9

Dolomite	20
Barium carbonate	5
Flint	28
China clay	6

A transparent base glaze with white crystals in oxidation. In reduction a pale blue white, matt, opaque glaze. Do not overfire.

Variation 1
With 8% red iron oxide a brown red glaze results with mustard crystal formations.

Variation 2
With an addition of 2% copper carbonate in oxidation a matt frosty turquoise glaze results on porcelain, a pale clear with green crystals on stoneware.

AS GLAZE NICE PULLED AWAY

381 Porcelain green speckled glaze   NICE GLAZE
LITTLE SOMBER

Feldspar	55
Whiting	10
Zinc oxide	10
Barium carbonate	20
Ball clay	5
Nickel oxide	2%

A matt, smooth, porcelain oxidation glaze, pale green with pale brown specks and brown streaks. Do not overfire.

382   Tan glaze with gold speckles

Feldspar	45
Whiting	7
Barium carbonate	10
Zinc oxide	6
Talc	4
Ball clay	10

Flint	18
Ilmenite (fine)	10%

In oxidation a semi-matt tan glaze with muted gold flecks.

383   Blue-green crystal glaze   *BEAUTIFULL ON PORC. △9*

Feldspar	35
Whiting	10
Dolomite	20
Bentonite	5
Flint	30
Rutile (medium)	10%
Cobalt oxide	1.5%

In oxidation a shiny blue green glaze with pale pink white crystal formations in a green matrix. Tendency to run.

384   Green matt glaze

Feldspar	44
Calcium borate frit (Colemanite)	5
Dolomite	7
Talc	20
Bentonite	4
Flint	20
Copper carbonate	4%

A smooth, dark green, matt glaze; a deeper colour on porcelain. Smooth greyer glaze in reduction, with slight pink speckle.

385   Chrome orange glaze   *BORING*

Nepheline syenite	10
Dolomite	36

Whiting	15
Zinc oxide	8
Bentonite	5
China clay	5
Flint	21
Chrome oxide	2%

A matt, opaque, tan orange glaze in oxidation. In reduction a muted green.

386 Crystal pink brown glaze   *RED. ✳ NICE RED*

Feldspar	33
Whiting	10
Dolomite	19
Barium carbonate	5
Bentonite	5
Flint	28
Rutile (medium)	10%

In oxidation a decorative brown glaze with small pink-cream speckles. In reduction a smoother, decorative crystal glaze; on stoneware blue and cream colours are formed, and on porcelain pinker coloured crystals.

387 Holly green glaze   *to green for my bark*

Feldspar	25
Whiting	30
Ball clay	25
Flint	20
Chrome oxide	2%

In oxidation a stiff, matt, opaque, grass green glaze. In reduction a slightly broken rich holly green colour.

388   Green yellow glaze

Feldspar (soda)	27
Whiting	17
Talc	15
China clay	16
Flint	25
Nickel oxide	2%
Copper carbonate	2%

In oxidation a semi-matt, opaque, green speckle glaze. Without the nickel oxide and copper carbonate, a pale cream colour is obtained. In reduction a mottled green brown glaze; without the colouring oxides a pale transparent glaze.

389   Speckled brown glaze

Feldspar	28
Whiting	17
Talc	15
China clay	16
Flint	24
Rutile	4%

In oxidation a smooth transparent pale brown yellow glaze with blue flecks. In reduction a more transparent, browner glaze.

390   Green black matt glaze

Feldspar	38
Calcium borate frit (Colemanite)	6
Dolomite	6
Talc	20
Barium carbonate	8
Bentonite	5

Flint	17
Zirconium silicate	14%
Chrome oxide	3%
Cobalt oxide	2%

In oxidation a mottled black green, metallic, smooth glaze. In reduction a bright, smooth, semi-shiny, opaque glaze.

391   Orange red glaze

Feldspar (soda)	30
Wood ash	20
Standard Borax frit	8
(Ferro 3134)	
Dolomite	20
Ball clay	12
Red clay	10
Tin oxide	3%

A brick-red, matt, opaque glaze with white speckles; in oxidation a bright colour develops, more subdued on porcelain. In reduction the glaze is slightly shiny and green.

NICE
RED + *392   Dry turquoise glaze*   *BEAUTIFULL. PLAIN! ONLY FOR BOWLS*

Nepheline syenite	50
Barium carbonate	30
Lithium carbonate	3
Ball clay	8
Flint	9
Copper carbonate	2%

In oxidation a dry-surfaced, bright turquoise blue glaze, smooth on porcelain, more muted and dry on stoneware. In reduction a dark green/red matt.

nice bright turq. in ud. crackle on porcelain

393   Pale grey-green glaze

Feldspar	40
Calcium borate frit	10
(Colemanite)	
Dolomite	10
Talc	10
Ball clay	10
Flint	20
Nickel oxide	1%

A cool, green grey, smooth, semi-transparent glaze.

394   Dark shiny orange glaze

Nepheline syenite	60
Red clay	20
Ball clay	20

A high clay glaze. In oxidation an even, bright orange tan glaze. In reduction a rich tan green glaze with iron speckles on stoneware, lighter in colour on porcelain.

395   Yellow green glaze

Feldspar	38
Calcium borate frit	6
(Colemanite)	
Dolomite	7
Barium carbonate	8
Talc	20
Bentonite	4
Flint	19
Manganese carbonate	2%

A smooth, opaque, yellow green glaze on porcelain in oxidation. In reduction a smooth jade green.

---

396   Light ochre glaze

Feldspar	38
Cornish stone	18
Whiting	18
Zinc oxide	6
China clay	20
Ilmenite (fine)	3%

A smooth, pale ochre green, semi-matt glaze in oxidation and reduction.

 REDX

397   Opaque silky jade glaze

Feldspar	41
Calcium borate frit	7
(Colemanite)	
Dolomite	7
Barium carbonate	7
Talc	20
Flint	18
Bentonite	5%

A stiff, silky, opaque glaze, pale yellow cream on porcelain in oxidation, pale green in reduction.

Variation
Additions of 10% zirconium silicate and 2% cobalt carbonate give a muted blue-mauve

not muted but nice of colour

---

398   Matt shiny ginger glaze   *nice cracle at bse.*

Nepheline syenite	67	*colour not*
Whiting	15	*rosy abov*
Flint	15	*but very*
Bentonite	3	*of useful*
Red iron oxide	2%	
Rutile	3%	

In oxidation a clear, fine crackle, ginger coloured glaze on porcelain, a dry, stone, pale blue-grey glaze on stoneware. In reduction a rich brown-black glaze.

---

399   **Orange green matt glaze**

Feldspar	20
Feldspar (soda)	30
Whiting	10
Dolomite	10
Talc	5
Bone ash	3
China clay	22
Iron oxide	2%
Tin oxide	4%

In oxidation a smooth, matt, white orange glaze. In reduction a medium green with iron spots. Do not overfire.

---

400   **Ash green glaze**

Nepheline syenite	35
Wood ash	35
Ball clay	25
Yellow ochre	5

In reduction a rich, broken yellow brown glaze on stoneware, a more even green on porcelain. In oxidation a yellow speckle glaze on porcelain, a drier cream white on stoneware.

---

401   **Cream stone glaze**

Nepheline syenite	50
Whiting	5
Dolomite	15

Talc	5
Ball clay	10
China clay	10
Flint	5

A rich, broken, cream brown glaze in oxidation; smoother and darker in reduction.

---

402   Pale ash glaze   *for judith*

Nepheline syenite	30
Barium carbonate	20
Wood ash	30
Ball clay	20

In reduction an opaque broken glaze, yellow on stoneware, green on porcelain. In oxidation a yellow speckle on porcelain, too dry on stoneware.

---

403   Matt black brown with gold flecks   YAK

Nepheline syenite	70
Dolomite	6
Zinc oxide	3
Whiting	4
Ball clay	6
Bentonite	2
Flint	9
Rutile (medium)	10%
Copper carbonate	3%

In oxidation an opaque, black brown glaze with gold flecks on stoneware, pink brown flecks on porcelain.

---

404   Shocking pink glaze   *FANTASTIC*

Feldspar *KALI - POTASH*	35
Barium carbonate	40
Zinc oxide	15
China clay	5
Flint	5
Nickel oxide	1.5%

In oxidation on porcelain a bright nickel pink glaze when thick, blue mauve when thin; more muted on stoneware, depending on the thickness of the glaze.

---

405   Semi-matt light green glaze

Feldspar	60
Dolomite	25
Ball clay	10
Flint	5
Rutile (dark)	2%
Chrome oxide	1%

In reduction a satin surfaced, semi-matt, pale brown green glaze, which gives iron speckles on a stoneware body. In oxidation a more muted pale green brown colour results.

---

406   Speckled green brown glaze

Nepheline syenite	55
Whiting	12
Fremington clay	20
(Albany slip)	
Flint	11
Zirconium silicate	2

In reduction a pale green brown glaze on stoneware, more even crackle green on porcelain. Too dry in oxidation.

---

407   **White firing matt base glaze** *nice crackle on porc.*

Feldspar	50
Zinc oxide	5
Whiting	20
Ball clay	20
Flint	5

An attractive, cream-white, matt glaze, dry at a lower temperature range, more runny at a higher range, smoother in oxidation than reduction.

Variation 1

A With the addition of 2% red iron oxide a delicate, pale, matt, tan orange colour results, which speckles when thin. *YAK on Porc*

Variation 2

B With the addition of 5% red iron oxide a richer tan orange colour results. *YAK on PORC.*

Variation 3

C With 1.5% copper oxide a pale green matt glaze with black speckles results. *nice to runny. + crackle*

* * *

Crystalline, decorative and local reduction glazes

---

408   **White crystal glaze**

Alkaline leadless frit (Ferro 3110)	43
Zinc oxide	30
Bentonite	5
Flint	17
Titanium dioxide	5

In oxidation a semi-clear glaze with white and cream crystals on porcelain, cream and orange crystals on stoneware. In reduction a mottled blue-grey glaze.

---

409   Pale pink (oxidation, local reduction) glaze

~~HOT~~ INTERESTING TO ME.

Feldspar (soda)	50
Whiting	15
Talc	6
Zinc oxide	6
China clay	7
Flint	16
Tin oxide	1%
Copper oxide	1%
Silicon carbide	0.5%

A muted pale pink green glaze with a chun effect.

Variation
With 2% red iron oxide instead of the 1% copper oxide, an olive green semi-transparent glaze results.

on porc. very bubbly yuk.

⚡410   Smooth clear base glaze for local reduction effects

Feldspar (soda)	35
Calcium borate frit	10
(Colemanite)	
Whiting	15
China clay	5
Flint	35

A smooth clear base glaze in oxidation and reduction which responds well to the addition of colouring oxides.

Variation: Clotted blood red   *BEAUTIFUL A g PORC*
With additions of 1% tin oxide, 0.5% copper carbonate and 0.5% silicon carbide a frothy red-blue glaze results; not suitable for reduction.

BUT RUNNY

411   Clear base glaze for local reduction *nice glaze A*

Feldspar (soda)	50
Calcium borate frit (Colemanite)	10
Whiting	15
China clay	5
Flint	20

In oxidation a clear base glaze which gives good reaction to local reduction effects. It is not suitable for reduction.

A *Variation 1: Frankenstein red*
With additions of 1% tin oxide, 0.5% copper carbonate and 0.5% silicon carbide (fine), a pale green streaky blood red glaze is obtained. Do not overfire.

Variation 2: Celadon green
With the addition of 1% tin oxide, 2% red iron oxide and 0.5% silicon carbide (fine), a pale medium celadon green colour is obtained.

412   Lepidolite experimental glaze

Lepidolite	50
Barium carbonate	20
Whiting	5
Ball clay	10
Flint	15

A matt, decorative glaze, best fired in oxidation. Smoothest on porcelain with a tendency to bubble on stoneware. The lithium content gives good colour response.

Variation 1
With 1% nickel oxide a pale grey pink colour is obtained.

Variation 2
With 1% copper oxide a rich pale turquoise colour is obtained.

Variation 3
With 1% manganese oxide a pale pink is obtained.

413   Crystalline green glaze *, boring* 7

Nepheline syenite	73
Zinc oxide	5
Dolomite	5
Whiting	5
Bentonite	5
Flint	7
Copper carbonate	2%
Cobalt oxide	1%
Rutile (medium)	10%

A crystal glaze: runny if overfired or applied too thickly. In oxidation it has a pale grass green transparent matrix with matt green crystals on porcelain, more silky matt on stoneware.

414   Speckled green crystal glaze *NICE GLAZE A 9 PORC*

Feldspar	38
Dolomite	6
Calcium borate frit	6
(Colemanite)	
Talc	20
Barium carbonate	8
Bentonite	4
Flint	18
Cobalt oxide	2%
Rutile (medium)	15%

A crystalline glaze caused by a high amount of rutile, which gives it a tendency to run. It produces a dark green glaze with a network of fine, light green crystals.

415   Dark green crystal glaze

Feldspar	35
Calcium borate frit	6

(Colemanite)

Whiting	7
Barium carbonate	7
Dolomite	6
Talc	18
Bentonite	4
Flint	17
Rutile (medium)	12%
Cobalt oxide	1%
Manganese carbonate	2%

A dark green silver crystal glaze with fine crystal development. It has a tendency to run; do not overfire or apply too thickly.

416   Silver green glaze   *NICE GLAZE ON PORC LITE DARK*

Feldspar	35
Whiting	10
Dolomite	20
Bentonite	5
Flint	30
Rutile (dark)	18%
Nickel oxide	2%
Zirconium silicate	15%
Silicon carbide	1.5%
Cobalt oxide	2%

A silver lustrous green glaze with small grey flecks. In oxidation on porcelain it gives a good deep colour, but do not overfire. In reduction it gives a darker green.

RED   **417   Crystal pink glaze**   *VERY NICE OX EN RED*

Feldspar	35
Whiting	10
Dolomite	20
China clay	5

Flint	30
Rutile (dark)	10%

A crystal glaze. In oxidation a light coloured speckled glaze with pink crystals, on porcelain larger pink crystals will form. Do not overfire. In reduction it gives a pearl blue-white glaze with white crystals. Do not overfire; it has a tendency to run.

* * *

Green, brown and black iron glazes

418   Semi-opaque celadon green glaze

Feldspar	35
Whiting	20
Ball clay	15
China clay	15
Flint	15
Red iron oxide	2%

A smooth, semi-opaque glaze: in oxidation a creamy green, in reduction a rich, muted, semi-opaque, holly green.

419   Broken red-yellow glaze   BORING

Feldspar	40
Whiting	10
Ball clay	8
China clay	10
Flint	20
Iron oxide	12

A runny broken yellow-red colour which gives an attractive 'ash' glaze in oxidation. It is too fluid in reduction. Do not overfire.

420   Brown transparent glaze

Feldspar	40
Whiting	20
Ball clay	12
Flint	28
Red iron oxide	10%

In oxidation a transparent glaze, dark yellow-honey running to black: a brighter honey colour on porcelain. In reduction a black/brown tenmoku.

421   Bright iron brown glaze

Feldspar	25
Whiting	15
Fremington clay	30
(Albany slip)	
Flint	30
Red iron oxide	10%

A rich brown black glaze. In oxidation a medium brown colour running black on stoneware; on porcelain a semi-transparent red brown. In reduction a bright iron red tenmoku glaze.

422   Black-brown glaze

Feldspar	25
Whiting	20
Ball clay	25
Flint	30
Red iron oxide	10%

On stoneware in reduction, a smooth black glaze breaking brown on edges. In oxidation a mottled black glaze breaking red-brown on edges. On porcelain a bright, transparent, dark honey-red.

423   Matt iron orange glaze

Feldspar	60
Whiting	15
Barium carbonate	5
Zinc oxide	5
China clay	10
Flint	5
Red iron oxide	5%

A matt, richly coloured, iron orange glaze. In oxidation a more muted colour on stoneware, a bright brick orange-brown on porcelain. Do not overfire.

424   Matt dark tan glaze

Feldspar	30
Whiting	5
Dolomite	20
Zinc oxide	3
China clay	22
Flint	20
Red iron oxide	8%

A smooth, dark tan glaze with black and dark green streaks in oxidation and reduction. Do not overfire.

425   Iron green glaze

Nepheline syenite	40
Whiting	3
Dolomite	15
Talc	12
Ball clay	10
Flint	20
Red iron oxide	3%

A semi-opaque smooth glaze. In oxidation it gives a green yellow colour, more ochre coloured on porcelain. In reduction a rich, speckled, holly green glaze.

---

426   Pale celadon green glaze

Nepheline syenite	25
Whiting	20
China clay	20
Flint	35
Red iron oxide	2%

A stiff, semi-transparent, high firing glaze. In reduction a smooth, medium green, transparent celadon. In oxidation the glaze is slightly stiff and bubbled on stoneware, smooth and pale olive on porcelain.

NICE
RED)
✳

---

427   Blue-grey celadon glaze   *MAYBY TO MUCH OF A CRACKLE*

Feldspar	55
Whiting	8
Barium carbonate	15
China clay	5
Flint	17
Iron oxide	1.5%

In reduction a deep blue-grey celadon, with crackle on porcelain. In oxidation a pale cream, smooth glaze on porcelain.

RED ✳

---

428   Deep rust glaze

Feldspar	30
Nepheline syenite	5
Whiting	5
Dolomite	10
Red clay	40

China clay	5
Flint	5
Red iron oxide	3%

A deep, opaque, rich rust glaze on stoneware and porcelain in reduction, with dry surfaces in oxidation.

---

429   Smooth green brown glaze

Whiting	15
Fremington clay	70
(Albany slip)	
China clay	15

A high clay slip glaze. In reduction a smooth, dark green brown glaze. In oxidation a paler brown, slightly dry.

---

430   Shiny smooth brown glaze

Nepheline syenite	36
Fremington clay	64
(Albany slip)	

A high clay slip glaze; speckled red brown on stoneware and porcelain in oxidation. In reduction a more metallic, rust-coloured brown.

---

431   Black brown glaze

Feldspar	30
Whiting	5
Dolomite	15
Ball clay	15
Flint	35
Red iron oxide	8%

A rich black brown tenmoku iron glaze on stoneware in oxidation and reduction. On porcelain a more mottled mustard coloured glaze results.

432   Even brown glaze

Nepheline syenite	25
Barium carbonate	10
Fremington clay	65
(Albany slip)	
Red iron oxide	3%
Rutile	2%

An even brown glaze, with a satin smooth surface. It is lighter in colour in oxidation, and more broken in reduction.

433   Dark red brown glaze

Feldspar	75
Barium carbonate	8
China clay	9
Flint	8
Iron oxide	9%

A dark red brown, satin matt glaze in reduction, a dry dull matt in oxidation.

Variation
The effect is slightly more broken if 8% rutile is added in reduction.

434   Streaky yellow glaze

Nepheline syenite	35
Whiting	6
Dolomite	15
Talc	12
Ball clay	10
Flint	18
Yellow ochre	4
Zirconium silicate	2%
Red iron oxide	3%

A streaky, yellow-brown glaze in oxidation and reduction on stoneware, lighter in colour on porcelain.

---

435   Rich brown black glaze

Feldspar	30
Whiting	20
Ball clay	20
Flint	30
Red iron oxide	10%

In oxidation a red rich glaze, breaking to dark green and brown on stoneware and porcelain. In reduction a darker glaze results.

---

436   Dark celadon glaze

Feldspar	43
Whiting	22
Ball clay	10
Flint	25
Red iron oxide	4%

In oxidation, a dark, mustard brown, transparent glaze. In reduction, a dark, rich, green celadon glaze results, brighter on porcelain and slightly glazed.

---

437   Orange green glaze

Nepheline syenite	38
Whiting	18
Zinc oxide	8
Bone ash	9
Ball clay	9
China clay	18
Red iron oxide	4%

A smooth, matt, orange green glaze. In reduction a more green colour is obtained, more orange tan in oxidation.

---

438   Green brown glaze

Fremington clay	70
(Albany slip)	
Whiting	15
China clay	15

A high clay slip glaze giving a matt, opaque finish. In reduction a smooth brown glaze breaking green; in oxidation a rich brown on porcelain and a pale drier brown on stoneware.

RED *

439   Tenmoku glaze

Feldspar	43
Whiting	10
Ball clay	8
China clay	5
Flint	26
Iron oxide	8

In oxidation a semi-matt black glaze which breaks tan-brown on edges and where thin; good on stoneware and porcelain. In reduction a more shiny deep black glaze which breaks brown on edges.

RED *

440   Green yellow glaze   *NOT NICE IN RED*

Feldspar	36
Nepheline syenite	10
Dolomite	12
Whiting	2
Talc	4

Barium carbonate	21
Ball clay	9
Flint	6
Zirconium silicate	10%
Red iron oxide	5%

In reduction a silky smooth glaze with a rich surface, medium green with a yellow speckle.

---

441   Muted olive green glaze

Feldspar	45
Whiting	10
Talc	10
Ball clay	30
China clay	5

In reduction a smooth, fatty glaze, muted olive green in colour, depending on the ball clay used. A dry cream grey colour in oxidation.

---

442   Sea green blue

Feldspar	65
Whiting	12
China clay	8
Flint	15
Iron oxide	2%

In reduction a pale sea green, clear glaze, with small bubbles and crackle. In oxidation a pale honey colour, clear on porcelain, a dry semi-matt on stoneware.

---

443   Green brown glaze

Feldspar	45
Whiting	20

Talc	4
Ball clay	24
China clay	15
Flint	12
Iron oxide	5%

A high clay slip glaze. In oxidation a stiff, matt, green brown glaze. In reduction a darker, black brown, semi-matt glaze which is dark green when thick.

---

444   Black tenmoku glaze

Cornish stone	55
Whiting	12
China clay	6
Bentonite	2
Flint	18
Red iron oxide	7

A semi-matt, black iron glaze, breaking brown in oxidation. In reduction a shiny deep black, breaking light brown on edges.

Nice fitting glaze to Brown for me but not a fall.

---

445   Iron glaze

Feldspar	70
Whiting	18
Bentonite	4
Flint	8

A semi-clear glaze, milky blue in reduction, stiff cream white in oxidation. Good iron colours in reduction.

Variation 1

An addition of 2% red iron oxide gives a pale green colour.

Variation 2

An addition of 5% red iron oxide gives a rich, transparent, dark olive green colour.

446 ✗ Dark olive green

Feldspar	60
Whiting	12
Zinc oxide	3
China clay	10
Flint	15
Red iron oxide	5%

In reduction a rich, dark, semi-transparent, olive green with iron speckles on stoneware. In oxidation a lighter olive green on porcelain, and an olive brown on stoneware.

447   Bright tenmoku

Feldspar (soda)	23
Whiting	15
Ball clay	28
Flint	25
Red iron oxide	9

In reduction a bright, gloss, black-brown tenmoku glaze on stoneware and porcelain. In oxidation a matt brown glaze which goes dark green where thick.

448   Black-brown vitreous glaze

Nepheline syenite	15
Whiting	15
Ball clay	50
Flint	20
Red iron oxide	3%
Manganese oxide	3%
Cobalt oxide	1%

A smooth, matt, black brown glaze. The high clay content makes this suitable to be applied to the raw pot.

449   Black-brown glaze

Feldspar (soda)	40
Dolomite	15
Whiting	7
Ball clay	8
Flint	30
Red iron oxide	8%

In oxidation a black brown glaze with bright yellow-green crystal formations. In reduction on stoneware a black glaze with brown edges; on porcelain a dark treacle colour.

450   Iron glaze

Feldspar	35
Whiting	15
Ball clay	10
Flint	40
Red iron oxide	2%

A smooth glaze, a muted pale olive green in oxidation, a rich celadon green in reduction.

Variation 1
Additions of red iron oxide give rich black-brown glazes in oxidation and reduction.

Variation 2
A further addition of 2% iron oxide (total 4%) gives a dark semi-opaque olive treacle in oxidation, a rich dark brown in reduction.

Variation 3
A further addition of 6% iron oxide (10% total) gives rich black-brown effects in oxidation and reduction.

451   Iron black adventurine glaze

Feldspar	30
Whiting	15
Ball clay	25
Flint	30
Red iron oxide	8%

A rich black brown glaze: in oxidation a brown and dark green; in reduction a smooth black brown.

Variation
With a further addition of 4% red iron oxide (total 12%) a rich iron gold speckle adventurine glaze develops in oxidation. In reduction the glaze becomes too runny.

452   Tenmoku glaze

Feldspar	43
Whiting	10
Ball clay	8
China clay	5
Flint	26
Red iron oxide	8

In oxidation a semi-matt black which breaks tan brown on edges and where thin; good on stoneware and porcelain. In reduction a more shiny, deep black glaze which breaks brown on edges.

453   Black brown glaze

Feldspar	40
Whiting	15
Ball clay	15
Flint	20
Red iron oxide	8%

In oxidation a red black brown, semi-clear glaze. In reduction a rich black brown tenmoku glaze.

---

454   Matt black brown

Barium carbonate	10
Fremington clay	85
(Albany slip)	
Red iron oxide	5

A wide-firing glaze: in oxidation a smooth, even, matt black; in reduction a light tan brown colour.

---

455   Mottled orange red glaze

Whiting	20
Fremington clay	70
(Albany slip)	
Flint	10
Red iron oxide	4%

A mottled, matt glaze, red yellow and brown in oxidation; in reduction a more shiny glaze.

Variation
Without the iron oxide, it gives a cool, mottled, semi-clear, pale green glaze in oxidation and reduction.

Appendices

List of Materials

The following is a list of the glaze materials used in this book, with American equivalents indicated where necessary.

UK	USA
Alkaline leadless frit (Harrison Mayer Ltd) (CaO 6.4, Na_2O 12.3, K_2 2.0, ZnO 10.9, Al_2O_3 4.0, SiO_2 56.1, B_2O_3 8)	Ferro 3110 (CaO 6.3, Na_2O 15.3, K_2O 2.3, Al_2O_3 3.7, SiO_2 69.8, B_2O_3 2.6) Frit 386 (Standard Ceramic Supply Co) (SiO_2 57.41, B_2O_3 8.36, Al_2O_3 4.96, CaO 4.35, Na_2O 4.21, K_2O 2.76, ZnO 10.48, BaO 7.45) Pemco P-991 (SiO_2 51.7, B_2O_3 5, Al_2O_3 13.9, CaO 6.4, Na_2O 9, K_2O 3.7, ZnO 10.3, BaO 7.45)
Ball clay (Hymod SMD)	Kentucky ball clay Tennessee ball clay
Barium carbonate ($BaCO_3$)	
Bentonite	
Bone ash (3CaO. P_2O_5)	
Standard borax frit (Harrison Mayer Ltd. (CaO 15.0, Na_2O 9.0, K_2O 1.2, Al_2O_3 7.5, SiO_2 49.0, B_2O_3 18.3)	Ferro 3134 (Na_2O 10.3, CaO 20.1, B_2O_3 23.1, SiO_2 46.5) Frit 550 (Standard Ceramic Supply Co) (SiO_2 50.52, B_2O_3 18.69, Al_2O_3 4.99, CaO 16.99, Na_2O 8.80) Pemco P-926 (SiO_2 50.5, B_2O_3 18.7, Al_2O_3 5, CaO 17, Na_2O 8.5, K_2O 0.3) Hommel 14
Calcium borate frit (Podmore Ltd)	Colmanite; Gerstley borate
China clay (Al_2O_3, $2SiO_2$, $2H_2O$)	EPK; Florida; Georgia china clay
Chromium oxide (Cr_2O_3)	
Cobalt carbonate ($CoCO_3$)	
Cobalt oxide (CoO)	
Copper carbonate ($CuCO_3$)	
Copper oxide (CuO)	
Cornish stone (K_2O. Al_2O_3. $8SiO_2$) (China stone) (Mineral flux)	Cornwall stone, Carolina stone, Kona A-3 Pyrophyllite
Cryolite (Na_3AlF_6 or $3NaF$ AlF_3)	
Dolomite ($CaCO_3$. $MgCO_3$)	
Feldspar (potash) (K_2O. Al_2O_3. $6SiO_2$)	Bell, Buckingham G-200, Kingman, K-200, Custer, Clinchfield # 202
Feldspar (soda) (Na_2O. Al_2O_3.$6SiO_2$)	Spruce Pine 4; Kona F-4
Flint (Quartz) (SiO_2)	
Fluorspar (CaF_2)	
Fremington clay (ball milled for four hours)	Albany slip clay

<table>
</table>

UK   **USA**

Ilmenite ($Fe_2O_3 . TiO_2$)
Iron oxide (Black) (FeO)
Iron oxide (Red) (Fe_2O_3)

Lead bisilicate ($PbO. 2SiO_2$)   Ferro 3498 (PbO 65.3, Al_2O_3 6.2,
(PbO 65, SiO_2 32.2, Al_2O_3 2.8) SiO_2 32.2)
                                              O Hommel 14
                                              Frit 28 (Standard Ceramic Supply Co)
                                                 (Pbo 65, SiO_2 34, Al_2O_3 1)
                                              Pemco Pb-700 (PbO 65, SiO_2 34,
                                                 Al_2O_3 1)

Lepidolite ($((LiK)_2 . (FOH)_2 . Al_2O_3 . 3Sio_2)$)
Lithium carbonate (Li_2CO_3)
Manganese carbonate ($MnCO_3$)
Manganese oxide (MnO)
Nepheline syenite ($K_2O. 3Na_2O$
   $4 Al_2O_3 . 8SiO_2$)
Nickel oxide (NiO)
Petalite ($LiO. Al_2O_3 . 8SiO_2$)
Rutile ($FeTiO_3$)
Silicon carbide (SiC) (Fine) (Car-
   borundum)
Spodumene ($LiO_2 . Al_2O_3 . 4SiO_2$)
Talc ($3MgO. 4SiO_2$)
Tin oxide (SnO_2)
Titanium oxide (TiO_2)
Uranium oxide (U_2O_8)
Vanadium pentoxide (V_2O_5)
Volcanic ash (Pumice)
Whiting ($CaCO_3$)
Wollastonite ($CaO. SiO_2$)
Wood ash (mixed)
Yellow ochre ($Fe_2O_3 . H_2O$)
Zinc oxide (ZnO)
Zirconium silicate ($ZrSiO_4$) (Zircon)   'Opax', 'Superpax', 'Zircopax'
   ('Disperson')

Conversion Tables

TEMPERATURE CONVERSION

°Centigrade	°Fahrenheit	°Centigrade	°Fahrenheit
1	33.8	90	194
2	35.6	100	212
3	37.4	200	392
4	39.2	300	572
5	41.0	400	752
6	42.8	500	932
7	44.6	600	1112
8	46.4	700	1292
9	48.2	800	1472
10	50	900	1652
20	68	1000	1832
30	86	1100	2012
40	104	1200	2192
50	122	1300	2372
60	140	1400	2552
70	158	1500	2732
80	176		

To convert °C into °F multiply by 1.8 and add 32.
To convert °F into °C multiply by 0.55 and subtract 32.

CONVERSION TABLE FOR PYROMETRIC CONES

°C	°F	British Cones	Seger Cones	Orton Cones	°C	°F	British Cones	Seger Cones	Orton Cones
950	1742	—	—	08	1120	2048	2	2a	—
					1125	2057	—	—	02
960	1760	07	07a	—	1135	2075	—	—	—
970	1778	—	—	17	1140	2084	3	3a	—
980	1796	06	06a	—	1145	2093	—	—	01
985	1805	—	—	—	1190	2174	—	—	4
990	1814	—	—	07					
					1200	2192	6	6a	—
1000	1832	05	05a	—	1205	2201	—	—	5
1015	1859	—	—	06	1230	2246	7	7	6
1020	1868	04	04a	—	1240	2264	—	—	—
1030	1886	—	—	—	1250	2282	8	8	7
1040	1904	03	03a	05					
					1260	2300	8a	—	8
					1270	2318	—	—	—
1060	1940	02	02a	04	1275	2327	—	—	—
1065	1949	—	—	—	1280	2336	9	9	—
1080	1976	01	01a	—	1285	2345	—	—	9
1100	2012	1	1a	—					
1115	2039	—	—	03	1300	2372	10	10	—
					1305	2381	—	—	10

The relationship between temperature and cones is a function of time and temperature.

For standard size cones, the squatting temperature depends on the rate of firing. When Orton Cones are heated at 150°C (302°F) per hour the above equivalents are approximately correct. With slower rates of firing, cones will be affected at lower temperatures. Actual temperatures are determined by accurately calibrated pyrometers.

Further Reading

Books

COOPER, E. and ROYLE, D., *Glazes for the Studio Potter*, Batsford, London; Scribner, New York. A readable and thorough explanation of how glazes are made and applied from start to finish.

COOPER, E., *Electric Kiln Pottery*, Batsford, London. A clear and comprehensive account of working with electric kilns.

GREEN, D., *A Handbook of Pottery Glazes*, Faber & Faber, London. A comprehensive discussion on glaze construction and ceramic science.

PARMELEE, C. W., *Ceramic Glazes*, Chaners Books. A scientific and detailed explanation of how to make commercial glazes.

WOOD, N., *Oriental Glazes*, Pitman, London; Watson-Guptill, New York. A potter's look at how the classical Chinese glazes can be made.

Magazines

UK

Ceramic Review 25 Carnaby Street, London W1V 1PL
Pottery Quarterly Northfield Studio, Tring, Herts

USA

Ceramics Monthly 1609 Northwest Blvd, Box 12448, Columbus, Ohio 43212
Studio Potter Box 172, Warner, N. H. 03278

AUSTRALIA

Pottery in Australia 48 Burton Street, Darlinghurst, NSW 2010

NEW ZEALAND

The New Zealand Potter 15 Wadestown Road, Wellington 1.

Suppliers

UK

Raw materials, frits, kilns, etc

Harrison Mayer Ltd
Campbell Road
Stoke-on-Trent ST4 4ET

Potclays Ltd
Brickkiln Lane
Etruria
Stoke-on-Trent
ST1 4PQ

Podmore and Sons Ltd
Caledonian Mills, Shelton
Stoke-on-Trent

Ferro (GB)
Wombourne
Wolverhampton WV5 8DA

Fulham Pottery
184 New Kings Road
London SW6 4PB

Clay

Fremington Red Earthenware Clay
C. H. Brannam, Litchdon Potteries,
Barnstaple, Devon

Chemical Suppliers

BDH Chemicals Ltd
Poole, Dorset BH12 4NN

Hopkin and Williams
Freshwater Road, Chadwell Heath, Essex
PO Box 1, Romford RM1 1HA

Depleted Uranium U_3O_8
British Nuclear Fuels, Risley,
Warrington, Lancs

Laboratories which will test for metal release
Harrison Mayer Ltd
Campbell Road
Stoke-on-Trent ST4 4ET

British Ceramic Research Association
Queens Road
Penkhull, Stoke-on-Trent

Ellis Testing and Research Laboratory
Aldbury
Nr Guildford, Surrey

USA

American Art Clay Co (Amaco)
4177 West 16th Street
Indianapolis Ind 46222

Westwood Ceramic Supply Company
14400 Lomitas Avenue
City of Industry
Calif 91744

B. F. Drakenfeld and Co Inc
Washington PA 15301

Hammill and Gillespie, Inc
225 Broadway
New York NY 10007

Pemco Products Group
5601 Eastern Avenue
Baltimore
Maryland 21224

Leslie Ceramic Supply, Co.
1212 San Pablo Avenue
Berkeley, CA 94706

Standard Ceramic Supply Company
Box 4435
Pittsburgh, PA 15205

Rovin Ceramics
6912 Schaefer Road
Dearborn, MI 48126

Cedar Heights Clay Company
50 Portsmouth Road
Oak Hill, OH 45656

Ferro Corporation
4150 East 56th Street
Cleveland, Ohio 44101

Harrison Bell (associate company of
    Harrison Mayer Ltd)
3605A Kennedy Road
South Plainfield
New Jersey

The O Hommel Company
PO Box 475
Pittsburgh
Pennsylvania 15230

CANADA

Pottery Supply House
PO Box 192
2070 Speers Road
Oakville, Ontario

*Laboratories which will test for metal
release*

Pittsburgh Testing Laboratory
850 Poplar Street
Pittsburgh, PA 15220

Bio-Technics Laboratories, Inc.
1133 Crenshaw Blvd.
Los Angeles, CA 90019

The Twining Laboratories, Inc.
Box 1472
Fresno, CA 93716

Coors Spectro-Chemical Laboratory
Box 500
Golden, CO 80401

Ferro Enamels (Canada) Ltd
354 Davis
Oakville, Ontario

Index

ilmenite
uranium oxide